Culture and neighbourhoods

Volume I

Concepts and references

Council for Cultural Co-operation

Council of Europe Publishing, 1995

French edition:
Culture et quartiers
ISBN 92-871-2868-5

© Photograph of mural: Jean Raty

Council of Europe Publishing
Council of Europe
F-67075 Strasbourg Cedex

ISBN 92-871-2869-3
© Council of Europe, 1995
Printed in the Netherlands

CONTENTS

Page

4

Appendices:

Preface

by Raymond Weber
Directorate of Education, Culture and Sport,
Council of Europe

Rarely has an urban structure given rise to so much discussion as the one commonly known as "neighbourhood" - not even the town or city centre, whose fragility was not recognised until recently. "Neighbourhoods of what?", one is tempted to ask, at a time when towns are no longer really towns but instead an urban patchwork, and their centres have increasingly become museums, the last vestiges of a time when neighbourhoods were not yet suburbs and the centre was a town's pulsating heart.

It is at this very juncture that the public authorities are solicited and that the need for Europe-wide co-operation is becoming clearer. Are there not common solutions to common problems? The ongoing exclusion of certain categories of people from certain neighbourhoods, from city centres in particular, was very soon perceived as the source of the problems. Yet all too rarely were measures taken to halt the trend (and the speculation), and now we can all read in the press about neighbourhood decay plumbing new depths and about the hotbeds of social conflict, and we see the violence on our television screens. The very names of certain neighbourhoods have become known beyond their borders as synonyms of social unrest because of their high rates of unemployment, drug use, insecurity and crime. Over the past few years, certain neighbourhoods have also been the scene of social and racial intolerance and exclusion, and no system of social protection or therapy has yet proved capable of restoring confidence in the ability of these urban communities to overcome their problems.

Having investigated over some fifteen years the topic of "Culture and towns, culture and regions", the Council of Europe (and through it cultural policy-makers from more than 40 countries) has set out to find its own answers. The "Culture and Neighbourhoods" project was born of this work, and we submit herewith an initial outcome for the reader's consideration.

We thought it important to emphasise that the neighbourhood has always served as the focal point for urban interaction, whether of a positive or a negative kind. Local action groups, exchanges between generations, community activities and environmental projects often find a natural setting in this unique cell of community life. One of the first theoreticians in Europe to study the "psychology of space", Abraham Moles, saw the neighbourhood as "the basic locus of spontaneity in social relationships, the primary meeting place, the charismatic terrain *par excellence*, the successor of the village in urban space". And, he continues, the neighbourhood is not only the place for interaction, but also that of social control. It is perhaps in this duality that the fault line appears, and we would be happy to say that all our efforts are directed towards enhancing the first of these aspects and reducing the weight of the second. In the area of culture, which in a sense is emblematic of this interaction, grassroots initiative has yielded many proposals and innovations, particularly in music and the visual arts. So-called community-based communication has been well received, and many neighbourhoods throughout Europe have followed suit, thereby making an important contribution to the democratisation of the media. In other words, we are much more inclined to regard the neighbourhood as a potential setting for the creation and construction of a European cultural identity than as a ghetto, with all its anxieties and controls.

The first results of the project presented in this book focus on a number of technical and political proposals that tend to bear out this assertion. Three main points deserve to be underlined. First, there are neighbourhoods in East and West, North and South, that are prepared to take the administration of their cultural life into their own hands. Successful examples are currently being looked at and will be the subject of a wide-ranging debate to be organised with the Congress of Local and Regional Authorities of Europe. Secondly, the neighbourhood must be the basic unit of all European policy. Selected neighbourhoods must provide the launching pad for European integration - still a laborious undertaking. Finally, it is precisely in places where daily interaction is imperilled by exclusion and intolerance that exchanges between different neighbourhoods and regions must be encouraged. Here again a number of measures are currently being devised, and others, supplementing this book, will be proposed by the "Culture and Neighbourhoods" project, which is to draw to a close at the end of 1996. Above all, however, it will have generated a wealth of information on the cultural policies of neighbourhoods. It is on the basis of these policies that other towns and cities, and other neighbourhoods, may wish to pursue this exercise and thus help to strike the new balance that we advocate.

I Introduction

by Eduard Delgado
Project Director

The present publication is the first of a five-volume series planned to describe the results of the "Culture and Neighbourhoods" project undertaken by the Council for Cultural Co-operation.[1] The project has so far made progress in developing the knowledge-base necessary to fulfil its objectives. Surveys have been carried out in 23 European neighbourhoods, oral history interviews have been recorded and policy data has been obtained from city administrations. But besides these useful fact-finding exercices, the "task force" responsible for the project has attempted to summarise existing state-of-the-art knowledge on some applicable theories of urban and cultural development. To this end two seminars were held with the purpose of unifying criteria and exchanging conceptual and methodological ideas.

The present volume sets out the general and conceptual framework for the "Culture and Neighbourhoods" project and assembles some of the contributions and results of the two conferences held on "The Urban Space and Cultural Policies", in Munich, January 1994 and on "Urban Regeneration in European Neighbourhoods", in Bilbao, June 1994, as well as a bibliography on culture and neighbourhoods and an appendix presenting useful information and addresses.

---

[1] Subsequent volumes will present respectively: a compilation of neighbourhood life-histories, a compilation of neighbourhood monographs and an analysis of the case-studies made. The latter would involve an assessment of cultural policies and strategies for neighbourhoods and include relevant information, policy proposals and action plans, which might prove useful for other cities. The fifth volume will include studies on specific aspects of interest such as decentralisation policies, interculturalism, local identities or cultural policies for segregated neighbourhoods.

The Munich Seminar borrowed heavily from existing sociological tenets on micro-urban analysis and the role of social dynamics in cultural development. The Bilbao exercise had as its main aim to link policies for urban regeneration to cultural policies and examine their possible impact in urban neighbourhoods. In both cases, participants had a chance to visit neighbourhoods involved in the project.

The two seminars nevertheless left many questions unanswered since operational consensus does not always suffice to make sense of social realities. The project has found it difficult, for instance, to reach a satisfactory definition of the notion of urban neighbourhood. There have also been enriching and stimulating differences in the definition of development at such micro-territorial levels. Some tended to consider the neighbourhood as a globality of phenomena: economic, political and social. In contrast, others limited the significance of neighbourhood realities to certain social and educational processes. Much debate was held around the notion of comparability in neighbourhood social patterns; the fact that 12 cities from as many different countries are represented in the project (plus complementary data from the "task force"), raises many questions on structural differences which hamper comparability.

Both seminars addressed the traditional divide between centre and periphery and arts versus socio-cultural policies. Here, discussions have been pointing insistently towards new ways of "reading" the cultural city whereby neighbourhoods play a number of different and integrated roles. It is expected that in this respect, the project will offer interesting insights into present situations and future scenarios.

As regards policy (rather linked to the Bilbao discussions), views differed in relation to the interactive dynamics between neighbourhood and metropolis. The models of city planning do not always help cultural policy decisions. City planning is supposed to take into account micro-surgical interventions together with macro-needs in the structure of the built environment. However, the way city planning tends to "resolve" conflict between micro- and macro-planning needs is very different from the way cultural policy decisions try to strike a balance between neighbourhood and city. If policies are built around conflicts on priorities no doctrine has been set out on the role of neighbourhoods in these conflicts. However, it is clear that the old opposition between centre and periphery or between arts and socio-cultural processes no longer represent reality in contemporary European cities. Cultural policy conflict in European urban neighbourhoods presents itself under a variety of forms and tends to require more sophisticated responses than those usually supplied for urban planning transactions.

The subject being a complex one, it seems that it needs to be addressed in a multifaceted way, which is the reason for the heterogenity of contributions and theoretical positions presented in this volume.

II Concepts and Projects around Culture and Neighbourhoods

by Franco Bianchini and Massimo Torrigiani
Department of English, Media and Cultural Studies,
School of Arts and Humanities, De Montfort University
(Leicester, United Kingdom)

> *Evidemment on pourrait fonder un orchestre, ou faire du théâtre dans la rue. Animer, comme on dit, le quartier. Souder ensemble les gens d'une rue ou d'un groupe de rues par autre chose qu'une simple connivence, mais une exigence ou un combat.*
> (Perec, 1984, p. 80).

This review forms part of the "Culture and Neighbourhoods" project, initiated by the Council for Cultural Co-operation, Council of Europe. Its purpose is to act as background material to support the process of researching case-studies in the twelve cities involved in the project, and, at a later stage, to assist in the analysis and interpretation of research findings.

The chapter consists of three main elements:

1. a **survey** of the objectives, methodologies and outcomes of relevant action research projects;

2. a **glossary** of "neighbourhood" and associated terms;

3. a **summary** of studies analyzing the main characteristics of the contemporary socio-economic conditions of west European neighbourhoods, and some observations on the existing and potential contribution of cultural resources and policies to the social, economic, environmental and cultural development of these areas;

1. A survey of action research projects

Our survey focuses on four initiatives:

▸ The first is **Banlieues '89** which originated shortly after the Socialist election victory in France in 1981. It was the brainchild of two architects: Roland Castro and Michel Cantal-Dupart. The aim of the project was to improve the quality of modernist housing estates, located in the suburbs of many French cities, which are largely inhabited by low income social groups. The initiative took impetus in 1983 when President Mitterrand invited Castro to the Elysée Palace in Paris. This eventually resulted in official presidential recognition of the programme, with the establishment of an agency working closely with the Prime Minister.

▸ The second project is **Culture in the Neighbourhood**, which began in 1986 as an initiative of the Swiss National Commission for UNESCO, within the programme of UNESCO's World Decade on Culture and Development (1987-1997). The project aims to create a network of best practice and information exchange between participating countries. Six seminars have so far been held within the project. The first seminar took place in Baden (Switzerland) in September 1986. The second, on the topic "La culture de quartier: la ville revit", was held in Rüschlikon (Switzerland) in November 1987. The third seminar, on the topic "Cultural Animation in Urban Districts", took place in Männedorf (Switzerland) in December 1989. The fourth seminar, on the topic of cultural diversity and multiculturalism, was held in Vienna in 1991. The fifth meeting, on "The Infrastructure for Neighbourhood Culture", was held in Helsinki in September 1992 and was organised by the Finnish National Commission for UNESCO in conjunction with the Association of Finnish Cities and the City of Helsinki. The Helsinki seminar also produced a working definition of the main characteristics of culture in the neighbourhood. The sixth seminar was held in Karlskrona

(Sweden) in August 1993. It considered examples of neighbourhood-based cultural policies in Sweden. The seventh seminar on questions of multiculturalism was held in November 1994 in Unna (Germany) and the eighth expert meeting took place in May 1995 in Tallinn, Estonia.

► The third project is **Quartiers en crise**, an experimental exchange programme started in 1989 with the involvement of relevant professionals and residents from ten towns and cities in five West European countries: Belgium, France, Germany, the Netherlands and the UK. The project was initially jointly funded by the European Regional Development Fund and participating local authorities. According to the first issue of *Quartiers en Crise News*, published in October 1991, the aim of the project is to build a network connecting European local authorities committed to dealing with deprivation and decline in parts of the urban community. The exchange programme focuses on an integrated approach to urban areas in decline (for example by co-ordinating economic, social, education, training, environmental, planning, and cultural policies) as being the most successful way of improving the living conditions of people in these areas. The pilot programme of Quartiers en crise ended in 1990 with a conference in Brussels. At the same time, preparations began, for a second programme, enlarging the number of participating countries to 10 (with the inclusion of Greece, Ireland, Italy, Portugal and Spain) and the number of participating towns and cities to 25. This was succeeded by a third programme, which is jointly funded by Directorate General V of the European Commission and participating local authorities, and is due to end in February 1995. It involves 30 towns from 11 countries. All European Union member states are involved, with the exception of Luxembourg. The approach and objectives of the project have not changed since its inception.

► The fourth project is **Banlieues d'Europe**, which began in 1990 as an annual encounter of individual artists and arts organisations involved in community-based activities and projects in different European countries. The annual international encounters have provided a platform for exchange of ideas about both the theories of using the arts as vehicles for community development and empowerment, and the practical aspects of carrying out work in this very diverse field. Artistic work presented at the annual meetings of the network has confronted a wide range of issues which are particularly strongly felt within deprived neighbourhoods: racism, xenophobia, religious and class conflicts, ghettoisation, the rights of disadvantaged people, the collective memory of minorities and the role of the media within marginalised communities. In April 1993, Banlieues d'Europe became constituted as an Association, with its administrative base in the offices of the Action Culturelle du Bassin Houiller Lorrain (ACBHL) in Freyming-Merlebach in Lorraine (France).

2. Defining the "neighbourhood"

Faced with the whole complex network of the city, entangled as it is with codes over which the user does not have control, but which he needs to assimilate in order to be able to live there; faced with the way in which town-planning has organized urban space; faced with the general lowering of the quality of social life within the urban setting, the user of the city, nevertheless, always succeeds in creating for himself places to which he can withdraw; he always manages to devise itineraries for his use or pleasure, which are the marks he himself has contrived to make on the urban landscape. The "quartier" is a dynamic notion which requires a gradual apprenticeship: by repeated physical contact with the public space, the user reaches the point at which he is in a position to appropriate it. The daily banality of this process, shared by all the city-dwellers, conceal the complexity of this cultural practice, and masks how important a role it plays in satisfying the "urban" desire of the users of the city (Mayol, 1980, quoted in Rigby, 1991, p. 23).

It's 10.30 on an average Thursday evening in a Welsh council estate. Some of the lads in the bus shelter are bored and cold. They've run out of the lighter fuel they've been sniffing all evening, so they light a few old chip papers with the remaining gas and whoop it up for a few minutes. Over the road, old Mrs Owens listens and waits in her bedroom. She's frightened to put out the light. The man next door hollers at them that his kids are in bed and don't they have homes to go to? He resolves to ring the council again tomorrow and complain about the kids and the bus shelter... It's just after 11.30 now and Arthur is too drunk to remember the number of Tracy's house. He takes a careful look up and down the street, takes a deep breath and bowls up at the house next door but three: "Come on Trace, love, I've got the tenner. Let me in Trace... Traceeee!" The situation is doubly unfortunate as this neighbour's daughter is also called Tracey... The mother...rings the police to complain about the racket outside. Next morning she is down at the housing department asking when they are going to get rid of that slut at number 67 and all her undesirable visitors (Castle, 1994, p. 82).

These two quotes serve to illustrate different realities of life in contemporary European urban neighbourhoods. A neighbourhood can be the "quartier" of La Croix-Rousse in Lyons described by French sociologist Pierre Mayol: "a local environment which is deeply satisfying on an everyday level" (Rigby, 1991, p. 23). But it can also be the nightmarish housing estate in the Cynon Valley in South Wales in which "a large number of tenants described the feeling that it was problems with their neighbours, anti-social behaviour and conflicts of lifestyle which governed their perception of daily life and consequently their daily satisfaction." (Castle, 1994, p. 83).

The two passages suggest that there is a veritably minimalist consensus around the notion of "neighbourhood": i.e. that a neighbourhood is simply a place where people live in relatively close proximity to each other. However, there is no consensus about the consequences of such proximity and, more precisely, about the quality of the human relationships proximity brings about. Therefore, it seemed appropriate for this literature review to construct a **glossary**, in alphabetical order, of definitions associated with the concept of "neighbourhood", in order to suggest to the reader the complexity of the term and of the realities it intends to signify. We are well aware of the fact that different terms used in different European languages to refer to the concept of "neighbourhood" have different origins, usages and nuances of meaning. It is beyond the scope of this paper to carry out a systematic analysis of the origins, development and current meanings of terms such as "buurt" and "wijk" in Dutch; "arrondissement", "banlieue", "faubourg" and "quartier" in French; "Stadtteil" and "Stadtviertel" in German; "borgo", "circoscrizione", "contrada", "quartiere" and "rione" in Italian; "barrio" in Spanish; and the Viennese "Grätzel". However, we do recognize that such analysis would be a useful exercise for a cross-European comparative project such as "Culture and Neighbourhoods".

Community:
"Community has been in the language since C14, from...*comuneté*, oF [old French], *communitatem*, L [Latin] - community of relations of feelings, from...*communis*, L - COMMON... It became established in English in a range of senses: (i) the commons or common people, as distinguished from those of rank (C14-C17); (ii) a state or organised society, in its later uses relatively small (C14-); (iii) the people of a district (C18-); (iv) the quality of holding something in common, as in **community of interests**, **community of goods** (C16-). It will be seen that sense (i) to (iii) indicate actual social groups; senses (iv) and (v) a particular quality of relationship (as in *communitas*). From C17 there are signs of the distinction which became especially important from C19, in which **community** was felt to be more immediate than SOCIETY..., although it must be remembered that *society* itself had this more immediate sense until C18, and *civil society*...was, like *society* and *community* in these uses, originally an attempt to distinguish the body of direct relationships from the organised establishment of *realm* or *state*. From C19 the sense of immediacy or locality was strongly

developed in the context of larger and more complex industrial societies. **Community** was the word normally chosen for experiments in an alternative kind of group-living. It is still so used and has been joined, in a more limited sense, by **commune** (the French *commune* - the smallest administrative division - and the German *Gemeinde* - a civil and ecclesiastic division - had interacted with each other and with **community**, and also passed into socialist thought (especially *commune*) and into sociology (especially *Gemeinde*) to express particular kinds of social relations). The contrast, increasingly expressed in C19, between the more direct, more total, and therefore more significant relationships of **community** and the more formal, more abstract and more instrumental relationships of *state*, or of *society* in its modern sense, was influentially formalized by Tönnies (1887) as a contrast between *Gemeinschaft* and *Gesellschaft*, and these terms are now sometimes used, untranslated, in other languages. A comparable distinction is evident in mC20 uses of **community**. In some uses this has been given a polemical edge, as in **community politics**, which is distinct not only from *national politics* but from formal *local politics* and organisation, "working directly with people", as which it is distinct from "service to the **community**, which has an older sense of voluntary work supplementary to official provision or paid service.

The complexity of **community** thus relates to the difficult interaction between the tendencies originally distinguished in the historical development: on the one hand the sense of direct common concern; on the other hand the materialization of various forms of common organization, which may or may not adequately express this. **Community** can be the warmly persuasive word to describe an existing set of relationships, or the warmly persuasive word to describe an alternative set of relationships. What is most important, perhaps, is that unlike all other terms of social organization (*state*, *nation*, *society*, etc.) it seems never to be used unfavourably, and never to be given any positive opposing or distinguishing term" (Williams, 1976, pp. 75-76).

"The term 'community', like other concepts taken over from common-sense usage, has been used with an abandon reminiscent of poetic license. In the case of some writers community has stood for those organic relationships that obtain in the plant and animal world and that may be found in human relations as well as between organisms of the same or of different species living together on a symbiotic basis. Others have referred to the community as a psychical rather than an organic relationship and have consequently emphasized consensus over symbiosis and collective action over the division of labour...

'Community' has come to refer to group life when viewed from the standpoint of symbiosis, 'society' when viewed from the standpoint of consensus. A territorial base, distribution in space of men, institutions, and activities, close living together on the basis of kinship and organic interdependence, and common life based upon the mutual correspondence of interests, tend to characterize a community. Society, on the other hand, has come to refer more to the willed and contractual relationships between men, which, it has been assumed, are less directly affected than their organic relationships by their distribution in space...

What has made the community an increasingly significant concept for sociologists to reckon with is, first of all, ascribable to its inclusiveness. It has denoted a series of phenomena ranging from the division of labour to collective action, from group life conceived in substantive form to the psychical processes involved in the interaction of personalities. It has thus included virtually the whole range of sociological interests from the territorial base to collective action, from human ecology to social psychology. In a sense it may be said that the concept 'community', through its ambiguous and varying definitions, has been instrumental in calling to our attention the fact that all social phenomena range between these two widely separated poles...

In the transition from a type of social organisation based on kinship, status, and a crude division of labou, to a type of social organization, characterized by rapid technological developments, mobility, the rise of special interest groups, and formal social control, the community has acquired new meaning and has revealed new problems... The change from status to contract, of which the trend from the family to the state as the predominant form of social organization is representative, and the change from a relatively high degree of local self-sufficiency to a delicately and unstable equilibrated international interdependence, best represented by the change from barter and local markets to international trade, finance, and politics, suggest a wider territorial basis for community life and the tenuous character of modern community opinion and action. The territorial character of modern community opinion and action. The territorial limits of modern communities cannot be drawn on the basis of a single criterion. Every important interest in community life may have a varying range of influence, and may in turn be subject to repercussion from without of an indirect and remote sort. The multiplication of corporate groups in modern times, the wide dispersion of the membership, and the increasing of ties of identification and affiliation of the individual with diverse societies often obscure the fact that every society is also to some degree a community" (Wirth, 1964, pp. 165-70).

"The existence of a particular set of social relationships which occur in a specific geographical location. These relationships are conventionally described as *gemeinschaft*, that is close knit, enduring and face to face, involving a high degree of co-operation, with individuals sharing not only common values and ways of life, but also common fates and futures. Together, these experiences and relationships generate what has been called a 'we feeling' - that 'we' are a collectivity rather than a series of individuals" (Evans, 1994, p. 106).

It is this *gemeinschaftlich* way of life - Evans notes - that is idealized in TV soap operas like Coronation Street and Eastenders, as well as in the rhetoric of politicians and policy-makers.

"Community as a term in common usage has a mainly ideological function. It refers to what people wish to believe did or should exist, rather that what actually does." (Evans, ibidem).

Nevertheless, according to Evans, the majority of community studies carried out in the postwar period enable us to draw some conclusions about the nature of *gemeinschaft* communities, and the factors which are likely to give rise to them. Evans summarizes the latter as follows:

"Social homogeneity... The majority of actors involved are likely to share some common social position and a similar view of the world, a homogeneity which might be based upon religion, ethnic or national origin, race or class. This commonality and consequent shared understanding is an essential prerequisite for the development of the kind of social relationship that *gemeinschaft* involves"

"Immobility:... A fundamental element of *gemeinschaft* ... is the inability to move which is likely to bind people to particular places. Those who are geographically mobile are able to move away from locations and situations which they find uncongenial. In contrast, the very fact that individuals do not have the choice and mobility to move away from problems in itself may determine a particular kind of co-operation and mutuality".

"The need to co-operate:... Appears to be a widely held assumption that human co-operation is somehow an inevitable part of 'human nature'. In contrast, a sociological perspective seeks to identify the cases and imperatives of social interaction... The need to combat racism in a hostile society may force co-operation among black groups; poverty, unemployment or religious intolerance may have the same effect" (Evans, ibidem).

"The answer to the question of whether communities can be created must be a clear 'No'. Nevertheless, ... there have been many attempts

by those involved in land use planning policy to create community...
The history of engineering for social balance goes back at least 100
years to the Hampsted Garden Suburb plan... Classical *gemeinschaft*
'community' follows from a high degree of social homogeneity as
opposed to heterogeneity. There is no evidence to suggest that
propinquity generates significant social interaction between different
social groups or classes. On the contrary, the typical response to such
circumstances is often conflict, social closure and 'encapsulation'...
Experience indicates that the social networks which may exist in any
particular locality are not amenable to 'creation' through public policy
action. Social engineering has a very poor track record, and although
it might be possible to argue that there are successful examples of
small-scale, self-selected communian experiments, the evidence shows
overwhelmingly that community cannot be created... The problem is not
one of 'How to build communities?', but rather one of 'How to
encourage stable and self-regulating neighbourhoods?', which is a
rather different proposition. It is certainly true that this latter objective
is more likely to be secured if residents have some degree of
commonality or social homogeneity. However, other factors will also
contribute towards this, including the need for residents to have a
'stake' in their neighbourhood, whether this be financial or social; the
requirement for inter-generational stability; the necessity of access to
local services and facilities (shops, schools, etc.) which effectively meet
local needs; and most importantly perhaps, the need to provide the
opportunity for people to have a real democratic influence over the
decisions which will determine the quality of their lives" (Evans, 1994,
pp. 107-8).

Ghetto:
"In modern times the word 'ghetto' applies not specifically to the place
of officially regulated settlement of the Jews, but rather to those local
cultural areas which have arisen in the course of time or are voluntarily
selected or built up by them. It applies particularly to those areas where
the poorest and most backward group of the Jewish population of the

towns and cities resides... Sometimes the area in which the Jews once lived but which is subsequently inhabited by other population groups, particularly immigrants, still retains the designation of ghetto...

From the standpoint of the sociologist, the ghetto as an institution is of interest first of all because it represents a prolonged case of social isolation. It is the result of the effort of a people to adjust itself, outwardly at least, to strangers among whom they have settled. The ghetto, therefore, may be regarded as a form of accommodation between divergent population groups, through which one group has effectually subordinated itself to another. It represents at least one historical form of dealing with a dissenting minority within a larger population. At the same time it is a form of toleration through which a modus vivendi is established between groups that are in conflict with each other on fundamental issues. Finally, from the administrative standpoint, the ghetto served as an instrument of control" (Wirth, 1928, pp. 4-5).

Kinship:
"The social recognition of a blood relationship or network of family ties. Kinship is one of the most fundamental structures of society, creating a network of rights and obligations and generating social cohesion" (Goodall, 1987, p. 252).

Neighbour and neighbouring:
"Who is a neighbour, and what is neighbouring in itself? Sometimes, and for some purposes, the answer to both questions may be quite unambiguous. The clearest instance may be where a governmental body uses territorial divisions within towns and cities as organizational frameworks within which inhabitants are induced into various activities together. Inhabitants are thus instructed what to do and with whom to do it; neighbouring is tightly interlocked with the overarching structure of provisioning" (Hannerz, 1980, p. 262).

Neighbourhood:
"A district, normally in a city, identified as a social unit by the face-to-face relationships between its residents. It represents a spatially bounded community and, while its boundaries are imprecise, outsiders are more aware of its existence than the residents" (Goodall, 1987).

"Urban imagery is one thing for the commuter executive and quite another for the slum child... or the vagrant with time, but little else, on his hands. Four are worth noting: (1) Neighbourhood is a very elusive idea. Intimate space is always restricted, though perhaps broader for working-class people than for the well-to-do occupants of suburbia. To the former; intimate space is a segment of the street, a street corner or a courtyard: this is the felt neighbourhood. To the middle-class suburbanite, intimate space may not extend beyond his house and lawn. As concept, however, neighbourhood covers a much wider area in the mind of the white-collar executive than in the mind of the working-class poor. (2) People, irrespective of economic class and culture, tend to judge the quality of their environment more by what they perceive to be the desirability of their neighbours than by the physical condition of the neighbourhood. (3) The imageability of a city, in the sense of how sharp and how many images are perceived and retained in the mind, does not necessarily improve much with experience. (4) A large city is often known at two levels: one of high abstraction and another of specific experience. At one extreme the city is a symbol or an image (captured in a postcard or a slogan) to which one can orient oneself; at the other it is the intimately experienced neighbourhood" (Tuan, 1974, p. 223).

"One finds neighbourhoods with mixed recruitment by way of work and residence... Here one may ask whether relationships linking residence-neighbours with work-neighbours ... differ in their role definitions from neighbouring relationships within either category. One ... finds neighbourhoods more or less wholly recruited on a work basis, such as shopping streets with shopkeepers and their employees as daytime neighbours" (Hannerz, 1980, p. 264).

"'Neighbourhood' and 'community' denote concepts popular with planners and social workers. They provide a framework for organizing the complex human ecology of a city into manageable subareas; they are also social ideas feeding on the belief that the health of society depends on the frequency of neighbourly acts and the sense of communal membership. However, Suzanne Keller has shown (in *The Urban Neighbourhood*, New York, Random House, 1968) that the concept of neighbourhood is not at all simple. The planner's idea of neighbourhood rarely concides with that of the resident. Moreover, the perceived extent of neighbourhood does not necessarily correspond with the web of intense neighbourly contacts. 'Neighbourhood' would seem to be a construct of the mind that is not essential to neighbourly life; its recognition and acceptance depend on knowledge of the outside world. The paradox can be put in other way: residents of a real neighbourhood do not recognize the extent and uniqueness of their area unless they have experience of contiguous areas; but the more they know and experience the outside world the less involved they will be with the life of their own world, thei neighbourhood, and hence the less it will in fact be a neighbourhood" (Tuan, 1974, p. 210).

"The area perceived as neighbourhood by the residents is often only a fraction of that perceived by the outsider as homogeneous social space" (Tuan, 1974, p. 212).

"What does, or should, a neighbourhood do for a citizen other than is done for him by the city as a whole?... The functions peculiar to a city neighbourhood, the things whose absence make a neighbourhood a less satisfying environment for family life, are these: 1) To give an aesthetic satisfaction, such is afforded by the character of construction - shrubbery, lawns, state of streets - all the things in the proximity of the home which give pleasure or the absence of which arouses disgust; 2) to afford safe access to an elementary school; 3) to provide safe access to congenial place spaces; and 4) to afford easy access to certain small stores and shops" (C.A. Perry, in Burgess, 1926, p.238).

Neighbourhood effect:
"That local social influence which is the result of a person's attitudes and activities being conditioned by his/her local social environment. Thus an individual's behaviour is conditioned not only by perceived self-interest but also by the opinions and images of other people in their neighbourhood with whom they interact" (Goodall, 1987).

Neighbourhood unit:
"A concept in modern town planning, ... of a residential area which has been planned as a wholly or partly self-contained unit, often with some degree of architectural unity in its design. It is based both on sociological ideas of community and the efficient provision of services. Neighbourhood units provide an environment for family and community life in which all residents are within convenient access of a primary school, a local schopping centre (neighbourhood centre) and open play-spaces. Typically such a unit has its own network of distributor roads and pedestrian ways and is insulated from the main through traffic of a town" (Goodall, 1987).

Non-place community, non-place realm:
"A non-place community or urban realm is a heterogeneous group of people interacting from widely scattered places throughout the world. Conventional distances are unimportant and accessibility rather than proximity is the necessary characteristic of place. As accessibility and communication improve, so co-habitation of the same place is not necessary for interaction, and consequently random and apparently untidy and unexpected arrangements of work and home can really be very efficient. Specialized professionals, particulary, mantain intimate contacts webs with fellow specialists wherever they may be" (Goodall, 1987).

The concepts of non-place community and non-place realm are useful because they highlight the fact that today, due to improvements in telecommunication technologies, physical proximity - one of the central characteristics of neighbourhood life - is no longer a precondition for creating interaction and building genuine communities of interest.

Residential segregation:
"The tendency of an ethnic group to cluster in particular residential areas. Any deviation from a uniform distribution relative to the remainder of the population in a city is an indication of residential segregation: the greater the deviation, the greater the degree of segregation" (Goodall, 1987).

Social network:
"The web of social interactions, comprising relatives, neighbours and friends, in which an individual or family is enmeshed by shared values or goals. Where a network is spatially confined it may form the basis of a community" (Goodall, 1987).

3. The crises of European neighbourhoods and the role of cultural policies

The contemporary conditions of European neighbourhoods have to be seen in the context of the wide range of economic, social and environmental problems facing European cities. This account is based on a review of available studies concerning West European cities included in the report *Urbanization and the Functions of Cities in the European Community*, by Michael Parkinson, Franco Bianchini *et al*, published in 1992 by Directorate-General XVI of the Commission of the European Communities. The report identifies three broad economic areas in Western Europe. The first is the old core, covering the traditional industrial regions of northern Europe, some of which have successfully adapted to economic change in the 1970s and 1980s by restructuring older economic sectors and diversifying into new ones.

The second area is the new core, covering the traditionally more lightly industrialized Alpine, southern German and Mediterranean regions which have benefited from recent economic growth in more advanced industrial and services sectors. As the report notes, "together, these two areas now form an extended core. The new core has not replaced the old core; rather the economic core of Europe has widened its boundaries" (Parkinson, et al., 1992, p. 49).

Beyond the expanded core there is a periphery characterized by relatively poor infrastructure, limited inward investment and a reliance on relatively technologically backward and vulnerable indigenous enterprises. This includes Corsica, Greece, Ireland, southern Italy, Portugal, Sardinia and western Spain (Parkinson, et al., 1992, pp. 49-50).

In the 1980s European city governments had to adapt to two related phenomena which had manifested themselves over the previous decade, bringing about profound changes in urban socio-economic structures: the globalization of corporate profitability strategies and the crisis of the 'Fordist regime of accumulation', which is characterized by large-scale production of relatively homogeneous commodities for mass markets. Technological change gradually made it possible for transnational corporations to shift unskilled and semi-skilled parts of the production process to newly industrialising countries, particularly in the Pacific Rim and Latin America. European urban areas whose economies were based on heavy industrial sectors, on mass consumer industries using mature technologies and on distributive services related to declining sectors were hit particularly severely. These processes produced reductions in traditional manufacturing employment. They also created polarisation in urban labour markets between, on the one hand, the better paid and more secure employment in the managerial, professional and technical fields and, on the other, employees - many of whom were women and ethnic minorities - in less skilled, low paid, low status and often part-time service occupations. Macro-economic pressures created by the recessions of the early and late '70s forced national governments to introduce public expenditure cutbacks, with negative effects on levels of public sector employment and welfare benefits.

Different parts of cities and different social groups within them were affected by economic change in different ways. During the 1980s in many West European cities there was growing economic, racial and social polarization, and subsequent marginalization of the most vulnerable social groups.

The clearest evidence of the unevenness of urban economic growth and decline can be found in urban labour markets.

The major trend in urban Europe in the 1980s was growing unemployment. National unemployment rates grew from the mid-1970s before levelling off and beginning a slow and tentative decline from the mid-1980s. In the same period, urban unemployment shadowed national rates but typically at a higher level. During the '80s, unemployment rates in major cities in France, Greece, Italy, the Netherlands, Portugal, Spain and the UK reached levels of 20% or more, up to twice the national averages. In some urban neighbourhoods and among particular groups the figures were frequently much higher, reaching - for example - over 40% and 50% respectively in some peripheral housing estates in Liverpool and Dublin (Parkinson, *et al*, 1992, pp. 119-120).

The growing influence of service sector employment in West European urban economies posed particular problems. Many service sector jobs - particularly in retailing, personal services and leisure - are relatively low skilled, low paid and short term. Substantial numbers of especially older and younger residents, as well as immigrants, were virtually excluded from the labour market. This problem is particulary intense in the case of ethnic minorities. Many working people belonging to

African, Afro-Caribbean, Turkish and more recently East European ethnic communities are trapped in the unskilled sectors of the urban labour market, with limited prospects of mobility, or, worst still, are being ruthlessy exploited as illegal workers in the informal economy. They are frequently discriminated against in education, housing, policing and the provision of other urban services, and suffer from the growing activity of racist parties and movements which have established strong bases in many European cities.

Economic inequities have clear spatial manifestations. Marginal labour market groups are frequently concentrated in particular neighbourhoods which are physically, socially and culturally separated from the rest of the city. This problem - found in new core, old core and peripheral cities alike - affects mostly two kinds of areas: the inner urban areas which have undergone substantial economic and physical restructuring during the 1980s and the peripheral areas which became the sites for social housing in the 1960s and 1970s.

Rising rents, land and property values produced gentrification and led to the displacement of lower income residents, which has characterised many West European urban areas, and has been particularly visible in capital cities.

In many towns and cities, provision of housing for lower income groups was downgraded as a priority by public policies which increasingly supported refurbishment rather than new building programmes, and reduced public housing expenditure by encouraging private sector redevelopment. Even in Denmark and the Netherlands, where the State and State-supported non-profit social housing associations have long been the major force in urban housing provision, there was a shift during the second half of the 1980s away from housing redevelopment for low income groups towards more costly schemes designed to encourage reurbanization by higher income groups.

London docklands - after the establishment by the Thatcher government of the London Docklands Development Corporation in 1981 - is an example of an urban regeneration initiative which displaced many marginal industrial firms and brought very limited benefits in terms of housing, employment or training to local residents.

A second example is Madrid, which in the last 20 years has become spatially divided into four increasingly separate quarters as office expansion and the development of high income central city housing has tended to displace low income groups to smaller, densely packed central districts where the provision of collective services remains inadequate.

Physical redevelopment in Brussels during the 1950s and 1960s also displaced low income residents and marginal businesses. This trend deepened in the 1980s as rising land values, property prices and rental levels encouraged more inner city residents to leave (Parkinson, et al., 1992, p. 138).

The establishment of certain parts of cities as 'cultural districts' also, in some cases, generated gentrification, displacement of some local residents and of some facilities catering for local people, and considerable rises in land values, rents, and the local cost of living - as measured, for example by the prices charged by local shops. All these processes appear to have been at work in Frankfurt's new Museum Quarter. A related problem concerns artists' quarters and other districts where there are strong concentrations of cultural producers. In these cases, the inadequacies of unrestrained property-led urban regeneration strategies become apparent.

Physical restructuring in the 1980s often overlaid and reinforced earlier patterns of segregation. Recent industrial decline in Marseille, for example, has deepened the long-standing divide between the poorer northern areas of the city and the richer south. In 1977 Marseilles's three richest *arrondissements* took 37% of household income whilst the poorest three took 9%. By 1986 the respective shares were 42% and 7%.

Pockets of regeneration occurred in some central cities which did not experience substantial economic growth in the 1980s. Dublin and Liverpool, for example, have had major waterfront redevelopments which transformed the physical appearance and, to a lesser degree, the economic potential of the immediate environs of city centre locations. But, many of the surrounding areas experience physical decay, economic marginalization, often with a deterioration of the quality of life of local residents. (Parkinson, *et al.*, 1992, p. 138).

The effect of central city redevelopment is felt by lower income residents in two main ways. Where public housing is less available, low income inhabitants tend to move to the nearest area where private rented housing is available and affordable. Where State provision of housing is more extensive, relocation to newer social rented housing, often on city peripheries, is more common. The former process is clear in Valencia, where the old city has become a reception area for those displaced by city centre redevelopment. The old city, containing pockets of severe environmental decay and relatively high levels of drug abuse and crime, stands in stark contrast to the nearby renovated city centre.

In many European cities, the provision of low cost housing is becoming a pressing issue. The problems vary in the three economic regions of Europe identified by Parkinson, *et al.* In cities in the periphery of Europe the problems consist primarily of rapid population growth overwhelming provision so there are both intense shortages and inadequate old stock. In many cities in the old core housing problems are found in the historic centres deteriorating from lack of investment and occupied by low income, often ethnic minorities, groups and in the massive postwar estates built in outer areas. In the new core cities, frequently the problem is that economic growth has led to rising land values which have increased the cost and reduced the supply of public low income housing provision. In particular, the peripheries of cities in Denmark, France, Germany, the Netherlands and the UK - countries characterized by strong public intervention in the housing market - often provide large-scale social housing developments. These estates, often as big as towns, are generally the result of discredited system-building methods commonly adopted in the 1960s and 1970s. Along with inner city areas, they house many of the most marginalized city residents, with fewest housing options available, and are often characterized by poor maintenance and the lack of social and cultural facilities. (Parkinson, *et al.*, 1992, p. 138-141)

In short, the most disadvantaged European urban neighbourhoods experience considerable multiple deprivation. Stephen Thake and Reiner Staubach, in their report *Investing in People. Rescuing Communities from the Margin*, published by the Joseph Rowntree Foundation in November 1993, identify the core elements of multiple deprivation in disadvantaged urban neighbourhoods in Britain and Germany. These include the following:

a) unemployment;

b) poverty;

c) social stress within the family: "many families with long-standing social structures built around male, full-time, unionised employment attracting relatively high wages are painfully coming to terms with the implications of women, earning relatively low wages in part-time, non-unionised employment, being the main providers" (Thake and Staubach, 1993, p. 18);

d) poor qualification levels and lack of basic skills;

e) poor health;

f) despondency and depression, often caused by long-term unemployment;

g) bleakness of the external environment;

h) lack of shopping, leisure and health facilities;

i) stigma attached to the external image of a particular neighbourhood: "residents are ashamed to admit where they live. They frequently find that residency in a particular neighbourhood is an impediment to getting employment, credit, and household insurance. It is not surprising, therefore, that there is a strong desire to leave such neighbourhoods. All the neighbourhoods in the study have experienced **rapid turnover and population decline**. Those who can move away to a more secure environment. For those who are marginal to the labour market - older people, disabled people and single-parent families - and the unemployed there are few escape routes" (Thake and Staubach, 1993, p. 19).

"Isolation, ignorance and adverse publicity are powerful contributing factors to the creation of stereotypes and prejudices. **Deprived neighbourhoods are stigmatised and negative characteristics are attributed to the residents**. These external judgements are accepted by many people living within the neighbourhoods. The decision to withdraw commitment from a neighbourhood is profound and requires massive changes before it can be reversed. For many of those who stay, expectations are lowered. Individuals, families and communities turn in on themselves, unwilling to trust or to form alliances with outside agencies" (Thake and Staubach, 1993, p. 20).

j) Social isolation from the mainstream of city life: "There is little reason for outsiders to visit [deprived neighbourhoods]. They frequently have poor transport links with the rest of the city and car ownership is low. With little disposable income there is little opportunity to travel outside the neighbourhood. The social isolation is frequently compounded by **physical barriers** such as railway lines, major roads/motorways, canals, swathes of industry or, in the case of peripheral estates, simply by distance" (Thake and Staubach, 1993, p. 19).

k) Thake and Staubach conclude that it is hardly surprising that such neighbourhoods exhibit "psycho-social characteristics of disintegration".

Thake and Staubach go on to argue that "multiply-deprived neighbourhoods are not associated with a particular type of landlord. Local authorities, non-profit companies/housing associations and private sector owners can all be present and any, depending upon the structure of the rental market, can be the predominant landlord. Neither are they physically uniform. Deprived neighbourhoods can consist of high-rise flats or two-storey terraced housing. They can be built of industrialised building systems or traditional brickwork" (Thake and Staubach, 1993, p. 20).

One set of conclusions from their study, therefore, is that "the inner city/periphery, religious/ethnic, high rise/ low rise, public/non-profit/private sector, old/new distinctions will shape the agenda and influence the solutions. They are not in themselves determinants of deprivation and their existence in a particular neighbourhood should not be mistaken for the central problem, which remains poverty caused by economic restructuring" (Thake and Staubach, 1993, p. 21).

Thake and Staubach's study continues with a discussion of community regeneration strategies which "consciously attempt to integrate physical, economic and social renewal programmes with the intention of establishing sustainable communities" (Thake and Staubach, 1993, p. 22).

How can the varied range of problems experienced by contemporary European neighbourhoods, identified by Thake and Staubach amongst others, be addressed through cultural policies?

Cultural policies focusing almost exclusively on city centre-based developments, predominantly aimed at tourists and higher income groups, have in some cases further alienated from civic life residents of deprived outer estates and inner city areas, who often find the city centre's cultural provision very difficult to access economically, psychologically and physically, because of factors such as the deterioration of public transport services and the escalation in the cost of out-of-home entertainment compared with its domestic equivalent.

These tensions were evident in many cities in the last fifteen years. For example, in Glasgow the cultural renaissance of the city centre - culminated in the European City of Culture cele-brations in 1990 - co-existed with continuing deprivation in the four peripheral outer estates of Castlemilk, Drumchapel, Easterhouse and Pollok (for example, rates of male unemployment in Easterhouse approached 40%). A pressure group called Workers' City protested against the 1990 celebrations, which it regarded primarily as a vehicle for "yuppiefication".

One way of addressing such conflicts in the spatial distribution of cultural provision would be to strengthen or, in some cases, create from scratch neighbourhood-based arts facilities. These should be genuinely accessible to all sections of the local community, and properly integrated with other amenities - cafés, leisure centres, libraries, restaurants, shops - to form "local centres" of activity. The city state of Hamburg, for example, established a system of neighbourhood cultural centres for activities ranging from rock concerts to language classes and political meetings. In Bologna, the city council - through its "Youth Programme", launched in 1981 - re-equipped and renovated the cities neighbourhood youth centres, with a shift of emphasis towards self-management by users. The Youth Programme encouraged young people to set up enterprises in crafts, computer graphics, electronic music, video and other cultural sectors. It built on informal skills and sought to bridge the gap between amateurism and professionalism. It thus contributed to reintegrating into the local economy social and economically marginalised people whose skills had often been overlooked by the professional cultural sector and by mainstream educational institutions.

This kind of intervention can be complemented by providing support for cultural projects initiated and run by grassroots groups. Projects such as the Festival Society in Easterhouse led to the establishment of the Greater Easterhouse Partnership, a body co-ordinating public, private and voluntary sector initiatives for the regeneration of the area. These projects are very important to provide an organizational focus through which community can express its cultural potential, identify its own needs and articulate a programme of action.

Changing Places. The Arts in Scotland's Urban Areas is a report commissioned by the Scottish Arts Council in association with the Industry Department of the Scottish Office, researched and written by Phillyda Shaw in 1992. It describes arts projects in Scottish urban neighbourhoods that qualify for special funding because of their level of deprivation. The report identifies a range of benefits of arts activities for local people. These include: enhancing community identity; improving the internal and external image of a place; creating opportunities for teamwork; sharing experiences; increasing self-confidence; acquiring skills; improving health by reducing stress; enhancing the physical appearance of a place; creating a safer environment.

The creation of neighbourhood cultural centres and the support given to grassroots activities could be accompanied by a strategy aimed at making the city centre - where most cultural activities and facilities are concentrated - accessible, attractive and safe for all citizens. Interventions such as anti-litter drives, signposting improvements, the introduction of "towncards" to easily book and access cultural facilities, the provision of more accurate and widely distributed information about city centre-based attractions and activities, as well as better policing, street lighting, late night public transport and car park safety are arguably needed in most cities to enhance attractiveness, accessibility and security for both residents and visitors.

References

Burgess, E. W. (ed.) (1926), *The Urban Community*, Chicago, University of Chicago Press.

Castle, B. (1994), "Here be dragons", in *Town and Country Planning*, March, pp. 82-4.

Evans, B. (1994), "Planning, sustainability and the chimera of community", in *Town and Country Planning*, April.

Goodall, B. (1987), *Dictionary of Human Geography*, Harmondsworth, Penguin.

Hannerz, U. (1980), *Exploring the City. Enquiries towards an Urban Anthropology*, New York, Columbia University Press.

Parkinson, M., *et al.* (1992), *Urbanization and the Functions of Cities in the European Community*, Luxembourg, Office for Official Publications of the European Communities.

Perec, G. (1974), *Espèce d'espaces*, Paris, Galilée.

Rigby, B. (1991), *Popular Culture in Modern France. A Study of Cultural Discourse*, London, Routledge.

Tuan, Y. (1974), *Topophilia. A Study of Environmental Perceptions, Attitudes and Values*, Eaglewood-Cliffs (NJ), Prentice-Hall.

Thake, S., and Staubach, R. (1993), *Investing in People. Rescuing Communities from the Margin*, York, Joseph Rowntree Foundation.

Williams, R. (1976), *Keywords*, London, Fontana.

Wirth, L. (1928), *The Ghetto*, Chicago, University of Chicago Press.

III Social Groups and the Cultural Regeneration of Neighbourhoods

by Jon Leonardo
Sociology Department, University of Deusto (Bilbao, Spain)

Second Project Conference on
"Urban Regeneration in European Neighbourhoods"
(Bilbao, Spain, 16 - 19 June 1994)

1. Introduction

First of all, I would like to stress that although the title of my talk is *Social Groups and the Cultural Regeneration of Neighbourhoods*, it is not a presentation by an expert on cultural management or a cultural professional, but one by someone who has had occasion to reflect a little on urban life in our cities and on what this means as far as individuals are concerned.

Consequently, my talk will focus on the following:

► First, I shall look from an academic point of view at sociological reality in the neighbourhood.

► The second section deals with neighbourhoods as key players in the urban development of Bilbao, with a few interpretative comments.

► The third section makes a distinction between neighbourhood culture and culture in the neighbourhood and in this section I shall mention a few ideas on the importance of culture as a factor for social cohesion.

▶ Finally, there are a series of thoughts on culture and the regenerating role it can play in urban life.

2. Neighbourhoods as a sociological reality - keys to interpretation

Since the beginnings of urban history, cities have been divided according to social classes, occupational groups or other criteria, and this has resulted in communities being fragmented into a number of fairly small areas, which have been the source of spontaneous local allegiances. However, it is only comparatively recently that there has been any analysis of the nature and function of these sub-units in the urban context.

Moving into the sphere of sociological analysis of the neighbourhood presupposes an attempt to unravel the confusion of concepts which, although similar in many cases, refer to different realities, not only because of the geographical unit they represent, but also because they relate to different urban contexts which for the most part have little or nothing in common. Consequently we come up against concepts such as *local community, suburb, slum, quartier, barrio, unidad vecinal, city-block, distrito, sección* and so on. All emphasise the importance of urban sub-units as factors in the building up of social relations, but they all differ in terms of the nature, limits and properties of the realities to which they refer.

Nevertheless, if we wish to look at the motivations, problems and social relations which have shaped neighbourhood life, in short at the sociological significance of the neighbourhood as a reality to be analysed, we see that these very concerns have made their presence felt in all areas of sociological discussion from its origins right up to the present day.

The profound conviction from various points of view that the new social order which emerged during the last century undermined the foundations on which community relations were built constitutes a major catalyst for sociological thought. Robert Nisbet alluded to this in his book **"The Formation of Sociological Thought"** when he wrote, referring to Comte, one of the founding fathers of sociology, "*Comte's sociological interest in the Community arose from the same circumstances which gave rise to conservatism; a break or disruption in the traditional forms of association*".

Similarly, F. Le Play, as early as 1887, was motivated by an interest in emancipation and reform of the working class and emphasised the importance of dividing an area up in a way which would conform to his wish to increase the level of structure and social integration of the society of his time. In his work *La Réforme Sociale en France* he writes: "*In order to encourage the return to truth which constitutes the very essence of local government, we must identify three distinct interest groups: cities, mixed communities and rural parishes [...]. Clearly, urban reform consists above all in leaving the inhabitants free to improve, through practice, many of the methods currently imposed upon them by legislation ...*"

In short, all these authors note that in order to come to terms with the city, which represents a new form of relationship and a way of life based on contractual relations of a profoundly impersonal nature, there is a need to develop areas of personal and collective identity which will give a sense of belonging, of having roots; urban sub-units are viewed by the authors referred to as something indispensable through which social practices are produced and reproduced, enabling society to exist.

For this reason, as a counterweight to the societal order of Locke, Hobbes or Rousseau, who stressed the importance of contractual relations in the individual-society relationship, there has emerged another type of approach more concerned with creating the necessary bases for achieving social cohesion within urban society.

Both the ideas of George Herbert Mead on the processes of the development of the concept of self and Charles Horton Cooley's theories on primary groups presuppose physically close relationships which facilitate the processes of social interaction.

It is not surprising therefore that both authors emphasise, from the urban point of view, the role of neighbourhoods, or more specifically, "unit neighbourhoods" as the key element in the process of socialisation, and hence, as a means of achieving lasting stability and identity. As Cooley himself states: "*In our own cities, large-scale housing projects and widespread social and economic confusion have inflicted grave wounds on the family and the neighbourhood, but the exceptional vitality they show in the face of these conditions cannot be overemphasised and the consciousness of the time was determined above all to make them once again healthy communities*". (Cooley, Charles H. 1956).

In more recent times, the sociology of the neighbourhood has been marked by a fierce debate on whether or not there has been a loss of community relations in the larger inner-cities. George Simmel warned of the danger of the fragmentation of the urban personality, the risks this represented for personal stability and the difficulty of maintaining total relationships in the cities. It was he who coined the phrase **blasé attitude** to express how urban life demanded a certain degree of ethical indifference which is inevitable if personal stability in the urban environment is to be maintained.

But it was Louis Werth who embodied this suspicion in his celebrated article "***Urban Development as a Way of Life***". Werth's central idea is that urban life is shaped by the development of a set of specific roles which necessarily dilute any attempt to seek community relations and therefore this entails the irreversible dissolution of local communities or similar entities as centres of social integration.

The whole of the subsequent debate among urban sociologists has focused on determining to what extent this is true. To this end, the theoretical approaches to the reality of neighbourhoods have been geared to the need to demonstrate the significance of neighbourhoods as centres of socialisation and collective identity.

Without wishing to give an exhaustive account of the various interpretations of neighbourhoods as a sociological reality, or to give an academic lecture, I nevertheless feel that it is important to put forward some of the theoretical points of view concealed behind this concept, which have the potential to form levels of analysis on which this daily and yet complex reality can be explored:

▸   First of all, some authors have interpreted the reality of the **neighbourhood as a place of belonging**, as a place providing basic solidarities which transcend politico-administrative criteria and inevitably give rise to a collective identity in the form of neighbourhood consciousness. In this interpretative line of thought we could include, for example, ecological theory with its emphasis on defining the reality of neighbourhoods as what has been termed the **natural area**.[1]

▸   Secondly, there are those who view the neighbourhood as a **social area**. This approach emphasises the importance of specific

---

[1]   On this concept see: R.E. Park, 1952, *Human Communities: The City and Human Ecology*, Free Press, New York; also E.W. Burgess, 1973, *On Community, Family and Delinquency*, University of Chicago Press, Chicago; W. Zorbaugh, 1925, "*The Natural Areas of the City*", Publications of the American Sociological Society, No. 20: 188-197; also by the same author, 1929, *The Gold Coast and the Slum: A Sociological Perspective of Chicago's Near North Side*, University of Chicago Press, Chicago.

variables as criteria of social differentiation and consequently seeks to identify more or less similar lifestyles among the population living in the neighbourhood. In this approach, the social homogeneity of the population is a necessary pre-requisite for the creation and development of the neighbourhood.[2]

▶ In more recent times, and adopting a point of view which we may call instrumental, there are those who view the neighbourhood as a **unit of action**. This model, as presented for example by one of its proponents Harvey Choldin, emphasises the deliberate and partisan involvement of the urban population in their local communities. It is a point of view which pays greater attention to the types of action which are representative of this form of community than to the ability to generate affiliations and spontaneous relationships.

In this approach, particular importance is attached to the neighbourhood as a unit which mobilises individual energies and efforts in order to manage its own affairs and deal with day-to-day problems. According to the advocates of this approach, the more or less formalised nature of movements, the degree of support on which they can rely, and the nature of their demands are the factors which give relevance to the role which neighbourhoods can play as catalysts and supporting structures of urban life.

This approach is reflected, for example, in the model known as **Community of Limited Liability**.[3]

---

[2] The pioneers of this approach were: E. Shevky and Marilyn Williams, 1955, *The Social Areas of Los Angeles; Analysis and Typology*, University of California Press, Berkeley, California; also E. Shevky and W. Bell, 1955, *Social Area Analysis: Theory, Illustrative Application and Computational Procedures*, Stanford University Press, Stanford (California).

[3] Harvey Choldin, 1985, *Cities and suburbs: an introduction to urban sociology*, McGraw Hill Co., New York.

▸ Another point of view on the neighbourhood emphasises the relationship between the inner city areas and the periphery. This approach holds that the neighbourhood constitutes the most genuine expression of **urban conflict**. As Marxist theory, for example, points out, although it is not alone in this, there is a close relationship between the texture of the urban fabric, its shape and its social inequality. From this point of view, the neighbourhood represents the spatial framework expressing class conflict and, hence, the contradictions which emerge from the various strategies for the appropriation of space. Most of the literature from the 60s and 70s on urban trends adopts this analytical perspective.[4]

▸ Another point of view is held by those who place emphasis on collective relationships: groups, associations etc, ie those who view the neighbourhood as an expression of **collective life**. For these authors, the neighbourhood, like any other form of human reality, is a collective work which reflects the processes of appropriation and production of social space by the groups of which it is made up.

Consequently, there is an emphasis on the importance of collective needs, which should not be viewed as the sum total of all the various individual needs, but as the average expression, as R. Ledrut puts it, of interests which may be generalised in accordance with variables such as class, culture and group. In this way, the voluntary sector becomes the genuine representative of the interests and personality of the neighbourhood.

The importance of the voluntary sector, whose various activities may be more or less formally structured (folk, sports, religious, pressure groups etc) is in many cases the basis for what is generally known as the neighbourhood consciousness.

---

[4] Christian Beringuier, 1980, "*Le reconnaître dans l'espace de la Ville: à chacun son quartier*" in *Espaces et Sociétés*, Jul-Dec, No. 34-35: 75.

► Another point of view which has been gaining in popularity in recent years is the one held by those who emphasise the importance of the neighbourhood as an area of **provision of services**. Concern with the quality of life, the importance of amenities as elements of spatial organisation and the growing disparity between lifestyles are some of the elements underlying the role played by neighbourhoods as providers of services, be they educational, recreational, cultural or sports facilities.

Provision of services which is structured around use of amenities gives neighbourhoods and local communities a unique role as privileged areas for the satisfaction of collective needs, as a concrete expression of the material and spiritual conditions for human development.

We should not forget that concepts as abstract as politics, society and culture are given a tangible reality in the consciousness of the urban population via the organisations and institutions which are based in the neighbourhood in the form of a community association, a union, a sports club, parish, civic centre etc.

I should like to end this part of my talk, which has been somewhat academic in style but which I feel sheds some light on the topic, by presenting the point of view of those who throughout the process of urban decentralisation stress the importance of **institutions**.

It is clear that regional/spatial planning in its various aspects (demographic, economic, ecological etc) depends to a certain extent on the collective structuring of space, one expression of which - albeit not always adequate - is the administrative and political organisation of the territory.

The view of the neighbourhood as an institutional framework brings out the close relationship between the neighbourhood and the organisation of political power. We must not forget that if there is one place where the close relationship between material living conditions and the political factors which make such conditions possible is there for all to see, it is the neighbourhood.

For this reason, the organisation of political power through district councils or similar institutions responsible for urban management and planning is a sociological fact of major significance. This analytical perspective also reflects the mutual relationships and contradictions which are to be found in urban management where local communities are concerned.

3. Neighbourhoods as key players in the urban development of Bilbao

So far I have given a formal academic presentation on the reality behind the concept of neighbourhood. However, despite the points of view already mentioned, which can be seen to differ in some cases, we should not forget that any theoretical approach to the underlying reality is based on an interpretative model which tends to downplay and simplify the infinite nuances of such a reality.

In the matter which concerns us here, the reality as it exists in Bilbao and by extension Spain, urban development has nothing or very little to do with urban development in other contexts; accordingly, realities which in some cases are referred to by the same names may in fact be quite different from each other. To give just one example, is it appropriate to use the concept of suburb/suburbio to compare such disparate realities as are to be found in the cities of the English-speaking world and in the cities of Spain? Quite clearly the answer is no; each city is the product of its own history and the circumstances which have shaped it and brought it into being.

A close analysis of the urban process in Bilbao will give a clear illustration of the complex relationship between urban morphology and human behaviour.

Furthermore, as is well known, urban development in Bilbao, and by extension in the metropolitan area, shows quite plainly the inadequacy of the various planning instruments which have resulted in a manifest failure to reconcile the good intentions laid down on paper and the harsh reality experienced by all concerned in the short term.

The urban growth of neighbourhoods has taken place independently of the administrative and political supervising authorities, which has meant that the city has developed in its own way, guided by markedly speculative interests, resulting in a chaotic situation from the town-planning point of view. Urban conflict has thus become an accepted phenomenon in our neighbourhoods and a clear gap has emerged between the inner city and the periphery, between the 19th century extension to the city centre and the more recent neighbourhoods built on alluvial land.

The history of our neighbourhoods is a prime example of improvised town planning, or tolerant town planning as some have called it. Because of the lack of institutional machinery for regulating the urban process, the "*invisible hand of the market*" was able to operate in whatever way it wished. The net result was that the neighbourhoods became a breeding ground for conflict and social protest.

Despite the changes in the living conditions in our neighbourhoods from the 80s onwards in terms of amenities and quality of life, the situation regarding town planning in the neighbourhoods was far from ideal.

However, although the history of the development of our cities might lead one to believe that this chaotic growth was a breeding ground for social disintegration and anomie, urban history has once again shown first of all that, academically speaking, it is inappropriate to interpret urban behaviour in an imitative and deterministic way, and secondly that the relationship between individual and environment is a complex one governed by the paradoxical nature of the individual him or herself, who is often capable of feeling and expressing contradictory needs and exhibiting contradictory behaviour patterns: introspection and openness, anonymity and individuality, symbolism and functionality.

If we look at the case of Bilbao, a deterministic view of the individual-environment relationship would have been incapable of taking in the tremendous vitality displayed by the neighbourhoods in the course of recent years. It would have seen them merely as an expression of the "non-city" or the "anti-city" as Henri Lefebvre termed it, demonstrating a virtually total conviction of the degree of moral decay which a damaged milieu such as ours can create.

It is not a case of advocating a masochistic approach or of implying that the more urban environments adapt to human needs the better they fulfil their role from the anthropological point of view. Rather it is a question of avoiding behavioural simplifications which lead nowhere and, instead, identifying what is good and desirable, together with what can easily be achieved and what is the most straightforward in design terms. In this way, architectural forms which at first sight may appear complex can occasionally be better adapted to urban requirements than can others which are apparently better designed.

In some places, plans which are often morphologically impeccable divest social life of its substance. In this connection, it may be useful to consider the views of an excellent author such as Jane Jacobs who in her celebrated work *Life and Death in the Big Cities* perfectly illustrates the error of urban designs based on the segregation of uses, a privatistic view of existence and, above all, a functional vacuum. Monofunctionality versus multifunctionality.

This is relevant because during the 60s and 70s, despite the obvious lack of all sorts of amenities, despite the problems concerning quality of life, neighbourhoods were, and I would add still are, capable of mobilising energies on an unprecedented scale, and in this way they have in fact acquired a multifunctionality which has served as a school for socialisation in its various forms - political, cultural and religious.

The neighbourhoods have woven a spider's web around themselves which has enabled society to be created and renewed, in such a way that the transition and acculturation of large numbers of people has been made possible in a city such as Bilbao, which in the space of ten years has seen its population rise by over 100,000.[5] This is a topic which has not yet been given sufficient attention and, moreover, Spanish urban sociology has confined itself to extrapolating analysis models which have little or nothing to do with our day-to-day reality. There have just been a few attempts in this direction, and in this connection mention should be made of the work carried out by the sociologist Eugenia Ramírez Goikoetxea on the importance of group relations as a factor in allegiances and solidarities; similarly, in the field of political sociology, Professor Gurrutxaga's study of the importance of oral codes as a means of transmitting nationalist culture, and the work by Professor Urrutia highlighting the importance of community associations as an instrument of social integration.

However, as I have said, these are the exceptions rather than the rule with regard to a problem on which much work remains to be done.

---

[5] The population of Bilbao rose from 297,942 in 1960 to 405,908 in 1970, representing a growth of 136% in only ten years. Leonardo, Jon J., 1989, *Estructura Urbana y Diferenciación Residencial: El Caso de Bilbao*, C.I.S., Madrid.

4. Neighbourhood culture and culture in the neighbourhoods

Having spoken a little about the role of neighbourhoods from the formation angle, I would like to say a few words on the question of culture.

Virtually everyone who has analysed the problem of neighbourhoods, their importance and the role they play in the city as a whole has emphasised their significant role as urban nuclei which encourage the social and functional integration of their inhabitants.

In addition, until a very few years ago, the vast majority of authors were agreed that each neighbourhood had a cultural substratum which identified and distinguished it, a cultural element which gave rise to what has come to be termed *neighbourhood culture*. This neighbourhood culture was nurtured by the network of associations and community life which gave the neighbourhood its identity and individuality.

However, if one dug deeper and tried to see what were the constituent elements of this so-called neighbourhood culture, and more importantly, to what extent this neighbourhood culture was homogeneous and produced a particular type of identity, it was at this point that the problems began to appear.

Ever since Louis Werth and his celebrated article *Urban Development as a Way of Life* stressed that the urban way of life brought with it an inevitable dissolution of primary relationships, all theory concerning neighbourhoods, local communities and urban sub-units has attempted to determine how true this statement is.

Consequently, I believe it is desirable when discussing the relationship between culture and the neighbourhood to make a distinction between two aspects which I feel are related but which should be treated separately for analysis purposes. I am referring to the distinction between *neighbourhood culture* and *culture in the neighbourhood.*

A. With regard to **neighbourhood culture**, ie culture as a set of standards, values, mores etc which identify and make up the way of life of a given part of the city, the following should be noted:

▸ First, urban development, or more specifically the expansion of the fabric of cities incorporating areas which at one time were both physically and urbanistically isolated from the urban centre, has gradually been undermining the foundations on which, culturally speaking, certain forms of neighbourhood personality were built.

  It could be said, although at the risk of being unduly schematic, that the more the neighbourhood has been combining its own urban fabric with that of the city as a whole, neighbourhood consciousness has been disappearing as a cultural and identificatory value of the individuals who live there.

  This is very clear, for example, in neighbourhoods such as Indautxu, where we are today, which have virtually lost their identity altogether and have become almost unrecognisable to their own inhabitants.

  This is why the majority of students of neighbourhood culture have gradually been losing faith in the role played by the physical environment as a place of attachment and a place of basic solidarities and have come to emphasise its validity as an area linked to the provision of services, be this in the form of amenities, a commercial area or whatever.

▸ Secondly, and as an addition to the last point, it seems clear that neighbourhood culture persists in a residual way in places where there is a certain degree of local homogeneity, be this for reasons of social class, origins, lifestyle or similarity of circumstances. The physical isolation of a given area can thus become a factor which definitely strengthens the personality of the neighbourhood; so that the greater the degree of social differentiation between the population in an area, the more difficult it is to rely on shared standards of behaviour, or a certain degree of homogenisation of the population, in order to assert its prototypical neighbourhood character.

Urban history is full of failed attempts to group together populations from different economic and cultural groups with the aim of forming communities, thinking that by simply reducing the physical distance between them it would be possible to foster a greater sense of community among the inhabitants. Very often the results obtained were the opposite of what had been hoped for: a closer physical proximity resulted in a greater social gulf. In fact, human relations are generally the product of complex mechanisms which are not necessarily brought about by simplistic urban development schemes.

▸ Thirdly, and finally as far as neighbourhood culture is concerned, it should be pointed out that neighbourhoods, like so many other elements of life in society, cannot be removed from the influence of ways of life and the resultant lifestyles. Contemporary society is formed and develops in widely varying spatio-temporal contexts. It is inconceivable to continue attributing to spatial entities such as neighbourhoods or the like, properties which they do not have; this would be to fall into the trap of a kind of absurd determinism, ascribing to space an ability to determine human behaviour which is not borne out by the facts.

A long time ago it was shown that the development of an area involves constant interaction with the individual, in such a way that the latter shapes the area and at the same time the area influences human behaviour. The neighbourhood will be relevant only to the extent that it is viewed as such by the individual, as something relevant from the point of view of his or her personal and emotional stability.

These considerations which I have put forward somewhat rapidly remind us that there are also several aspects of the problem of neighbourhood culture which it would be wise to consider at this juncture.

- ▸ First, in contrast to the determinism reflected in some interpretations of the neighbourhood, stressing its importance as an instrument of acculturation and inevitable attachment, its role and relevance are more the product of an elective process by the individual than an inevitable circumstance. In this connection, particular attention should be paid to highlighting the importance of the LOCAL, as it is called by Giddens, to emphasise the area in the immediate vicinity of the individual from which he or she obtains what Giddens calls a certain degree of ontological security. However, this immediate space does not necessarily reflect a specific physical space, but may vary with time and involve different spaces. People today have the same opportunities to form allegiances and belong to neighbourhood associations as to belong to transnational associations. Whether they belong or not will depend on an elective process which in turn depends on the need to give a meaning to their daily lives.

- ▸ This leads us to recognise that contemporary life is based, from the point of view of spatial anthropology, on a constant tension between the localised nature of our actions and the degree of universality from which they draw inspiration. The global village in which we live causes many individuals to be conscious of standards of behaviour and values which reach far beyond the immediate local surroundings. This means that the life of individuals is not predetermined by the immediate surroundings but in accordance with physically remote reference points.

▸ Nevertheless, the fact that the neighbourhood is no longer viewed as the only frame of reference does not minimise its role. The individual cannot live without a certain degree of rootedness or a sense of cultural belonging. Neighbourhood culture thus emerges as another reference element for the individual, changing its original meaning and offering itself as an alternative in competition with others in order to give the citizen's day-to-day activities a sense and a meaning. In this way the neighbourhood gives individuals a sense of belonging, but at the same time takes on a more important and more active role in so far as it becomes an area which provides services.

B. With regard to the second aspect, **culture in the neighbourhood**, the perspective is a little different in that it refers to the existence of means which make cultural creation and re-creation possible. Although it is of course related to what we have been discussing above, it raises a problem on a larger scale, namely to what extent should those fields of human life which are not directly quantifiable in terms of value but which are totally necessary for what not too long ago the Marxists still called the "*reproduction of social life*" be incorporated in neighbourhood planning and management?

Here we should bear in mind, at least with regard to the situation in Spain, that despite the multitude of appeals made from various fields, planning offers no guidelines whatsoever in this regard and manages at most merely to establish standards for amenities in a very general way without defining the types of amenities in practical terms.

It should nevertheless be noted that despite the fact that since the beginning of the political transition urban planning has been especially concerned with raising the quality of life in cities, attaching particular importance to policy on social amenities, these amenities have appeared in a very unevenly balanced way, depending on the type of activity it was deemed necessary to promote at the time.

In this connection, local institutions have developed an ambitious - and as far as Spain is concerned unprecedented - policy on sports amenities, but the same has not been done for cultural facilities despite the progress achieved.

Obviously, above and beyond the explanations of the policies carried out, the provision of cultural activities comes up against the problem of translating artistic categories linked to the process of creation, and the freedom inherent therein, into criteria for action which require a certain level of standardisation.

Of course, it is not up to institutions to dictate how art should be produced or how books should be written: the creative process is *per se* an open process of creation and re-creation of reality. However, in the same way as the right conditions for participation in sports activities are created, there is no reason why institutions can and should not provide the conditions of plausibility enabling artistic creation to become part of daily reality. The argument is all the more compelling if it is remembered that the process of artistic creation in the majority of cases does not require large sums of money to be invested in costly installations.

Only by incorporating the field of artistic creation in all its manifestations in daily life will it be possible for the neighbourhood to become a place where artistic experiences can be exchanged, making it possible to transcend the individual nature of artistic activity, and by extension the specific neighbourhood culture, to attain the degree of universality which every artistic work reflects through aesthetic enjoyment.

5. Culture as an element of urban regeneration

To conclude I would like to put forward a number of thoughts with the aim not of providing any ready-made answers to a problem such as the one we are considering here, but of suggesting possible lines of debate.

First of all I would like to say that in any discussion on culture and the contribution it makes via its various forms to the process of urban regeneration, it is advisable to state beforehand one's initial assumptions. I say this because there is a need to make a prior conceptual clarification concerning the sense and meaning of culture. If we regard it as an **exchangeable commodity,** ie an item which has some market value, then we have to place ourselves in the market context and try to gauge how appealing it is likely to be and what will be the probable economic impact. However, if we regard the process of creation as a **useable commodity,** an object to be acquired by the individual for his or her personal and spiritual satisfaction, we find ourselves confronted with all the difficulties inherent in such a concept.

Here, the impact of this type of activity is not so readily quantifiable. Its validity is justified in terms of the deepest aspirations and needs felt by the human being.

This difficulty with regard to measurability and incorporation into a productive scheme should not lead us to dismiss art as something which appeals only to finer feelings and a kind of old-fashioned idealism. Artistic creation is one of the best ways of achieving a greater degree of urban integration. The history of urban development is full of examples which show that those cities which were the most developed in terms of culture and art were the ones which achieved a greater degree of human development and consequently minimised the price which has to be paid for urban development.

There is no need to stress how important this point is, given the threat of decay and poverty facing our cities.

Secondly, it should be pointed out that as far as policy on cultural facilities is concerned, and with regard to the impact on urban management, there needs to be collaboration between different levels of activity, levels which are of a complementary nature, are inter-related and provide mutual feedback, but which should not be mixed indiscriminately. Their size, structure, role and activity vary according to the degree of attraction they exert and according to whether they are of a local, regional or international nature.

With regard to the physical infrastructures which support cultural activities as a means of regeneration, **versatility** and **accessibility** emerge as two important characteristics in the design of cultural facilities.

Only in this way is it possible to combine a variety of activities at the same time, making the installations profitable by making them available to the greatest possible number of people.

In conclusion, I would like to say something which has been underlying this talk from the outset. And here I would like to refer to Aristotle for whom the Greek *polis* represented the *good life* in the deepest sense of the term. Culture and the associated processes of creation cannot be a mere pretext for situations such as this. A firm belief in its role and in the beneficial effects it has for urban life constitutes an essential prerequisite if we are to achieve greater material and moral well-being.

Now that the crisis in our civilisation associated with quantitative growth has demonstrated the need to develop new possibilities of the individual that go beyond the logic of the market, cultural creation and development can be seen as supports and guarantees of a higher level of urban life; at the same time it is clear that we must uphold the right to be different as an inalienable right of the individual in the face of the standardising logic of the market; the difference which the act of individual creation presupposes can be seen as a necessary way of reassociating the individual with the group.

I would not like to end without saying that only by accepting the differences and otherness represented by the individualisation inherent in the act of creation, is it possible to create an integrated society at peace with itself, in which space is not a kind of straitjacket which individuals must fit themselves into, but the natural extension of this humanised environment which spans the period from the neolithic village up to the present day.

IV Building a Context for Neighbourhood Cultural Regeneration

by Brian Goodey
Urban Landscape Design, Oxford Brookes University
(United Kingdom)

Second Project Conference on
"Urban Regeneration in European Neighbourhoods"
(Bilbao, Spain, 16 - 19 June 1994)

1. Introduction

There is a deterministic implication in the title of this paper, that "building" - the creation of buildings, contained urban space etc., can provide a context for neighbourhood culture, and that such a cultural life might be "regenerated" through the arrival, form and impact of such "building". Certainly a number of matters to clarify at the outset!

Our preoccupation with "urban culture", certainly in the traditional sense of a tight-knit interaction of residents in the generation of non-economically based activities, is derived from a belief in both traditional survival and social control. We need, at the outset, to establish our territory in the area of urban culture.

During my association with the Council of Europe, I have been alerted to the common belief that the vitality of European everyday life is maintained by the spontaneous activity of local groups who (somewhat surprisingly) meet the professional analysis, and provide a ready supply of cultural activities. Contrary to the all-enveloping dictates of a multi-national, world-order, local communities are expected to generate music, dance, vitality and innovation which strike against the multi-media impositions of trans-Atlantic cultural Empires.

This, of course, is an **illusion**. Penetrate deep into the territory of the local neighbourhood group and you will find, not the perpetuation of traditional cultural forms (which have now been hijacked by "experts" and middle class admirers) but the rapid uptake of the most contemporary and future-oriented of cultural activities.

2. The age-family life cycle

This is tied to age and expectation, two issues which are seldom addressed in Council of Europe discussions. I would strongly suggest that we need to disaggregate our consideration of local populations into various age/interest groups. Such groups are not exclusive. Age is not the sole determinant of our interest in, and involvement in, cultural activity ... but it is the most significant.

As a target at which to aim, consider the family/age life cycle. The schoolchild between 0 - 11 is offered a wide range of activities and interests derived from parental and school values, together with parental expectations as to the future. The boy is made to dance, the girl is taken through a series of self-aggrandising but ultimately rejected activities. Ballet and band, little league and scouting are imposed, increasingly as an escape from the turgid bonds of family. By secondary school the educational context enlarges and during the teenage years the neighbourhood resident experiments, rapidly moving from any traditional activities to the seductive world of marketed US television spin-offs, pop record images and diluted work events; the age of music, sex and drugs, of inadequate moral structures and glamour opportunities. How distant is this from our image of neighbourhood urban culture? An almost total rejection of the past, with traditions and consolidated community culture abandoned.

If - and it is a big if - the teenagers survive, then it is a slow progress to a fixed relationship and domestic life - at anything between the late teens and the late twenties. A consolidation and, perhaps, the beginning of a reference back to parental tradition ... picking up the debris of decay and parental interests be they vintage motorbikes, record collections or knitting.

The implication is that at their most active, from eleven to the early twenties, community involvers have little interest in the community. It is stay-at-homes, the second grade, that stay in the area. By the late twenties the family unit may be in formation (but note the considerable range in fixed arrangements between European cultures). In the late twenties and thirties the family re-cycles its role in the community. Ethnic and regional antecedents are recalled as the next generation of children are put through the folk dancing and cultural paces, whilst their parents range the city and its region searching for retail opportunities and "days out". As the second generation of teenagers grows up, their parents may well have recourse to a local or district culture - unless they have managed to escape to a new residential area!

This thirty-year old involvement may be sustained into old - and these days very old - age and we are therefore talking about 30 - 90 year olds, established in a neighbourhood and requiring relationships which establish and maintain an interest in past culture, be it ethnic, class or interest based. Such a cultural involvement is likely to become increasingly exclusive, the demands of association making outsiders threatening and the context for activity being strongly maintained. The new generations will, of course, rebel, and reject the established traditions, which themselves change more subtly when assaulted by media, promotion and cost.

Whilst assaulted by political and cultural change, the age-family life cycle is key to our understanding of what activity will be supported by the local community. This is an under-recognised and under-explored area of enquiry, but is central to the ways in which local communities generate their culture.

Who are the movers and doers? In any analysis of local cultural life, who are the people who are making things move? Shaking the local authority, heading meetings, stirring up new interests, drawing on generations?

3. Why the importance of neighbourhood culture?

Clearly there is a set of value judgements which rest behind our concern for neighbourhood culture. There is a belief that each individual, at the neighbourhood level, should contribute towards the regeneration of a local cultural life. In combination with others in the city the resident stimulates a diversity which confronts the imposed, international culture of world cities, multi-media pop music, block-busting novels and mindless icons which comprise the gloss of international culture today. We have to believe that such linkage, between neighbourhood and district, district and city, city and neighbouring city, is possible.

Such a value position thrives on diversity, on regret for the loss of local and regional identity, or individuality, and on the generative force behind amateur (as distinct from professional) design. In discussing the potential for neighbourhood culture, in highlighting its opportunities, we are promoting a position which, whilst widely discussed in non-parliamentary forums, seldom features in national political debate or in international decisions.

Cultural diversity is an attractive concept for leisure consumption - for tourism development, marketing etc. - and has largely been internalised by the process of place selling. Seldom do we allow ourselves to consider the local impact of such support, and the realisation that support for local and regional identity is largely directed towards future evolution rather than preservation of the past.

4. The economic variable

This broad sweep stands well in an environment where all have equal access to opportunity and facilities, but this is clearly not the case. Access, distances travelled, events joined, all depend on purchasing power and on the economic positions of the residents and families concerned.

Overlaying the simple map of who lives where, and who groups with whom, is the more flexible map of who can **afford** to visit what, associate with whom, advance which cultural cause.

Given emerging mobility, those trapped in the neighbourhood are the disadvantaged - those who cannot range the city scene. Who are they?

They are the non-car owners, and those, in addition, who are unable or are afraid to use public transport. This can embrace a majority of the urban population - the pre-driver youth, the wives stranded without a car, and the elderly, as well as those who cannot afford either public or private transport, who are trapped in the local neighbourhood, rather than those who choose to use it for their leisure and recreation.

Here we are focusing on municipal support, on the convinced need by local authorities to support the cultural life of those who are unable to join together for other than basic maintenance. This provides the basic rationale for municipal provision, for buildings, staff, events and facilities which may be eagerly jumped upon by the well-equipped middle-classes, but which are aimed at drawing the trapped out of their homes.

In many countries, the 1980's have presumed that only expenditure, visitors, users, clients, customers, and audiences justify municipal support for culture. We have focused on helping those who can already help themselves, linking them with High Culture promoted and endorsed by national and international elites.

We must all ask how long we can assume that the poor, the aged, the "underclass" will be willing to circulate through the dregs of the industrial society, whilst the affluent and the mobile enjoy the products and promotions of the post-industrial world.
Within the present project, I see this as a key issue which we have not, so far, examined.

5. The physical environment of neighbourhood culture

Taking this perspective, how significant is the structure and design of the city at the neighbourhood level? In many cities the private market has been allowed full rein, with "uneconomic" public facilities privatised, the local restaurant turned into a computer sales centre, the local shop now a speciality target visited by car-borne metropolitan visitors.

This has become a universal European phenomena over the past fifteen years, with the expectation that the growing affluent will stifle the voice of those who have lost out in the market race. I strongly suspect that by the end of the century, this easy-going agenda will not be sustainable by local or national politicians. Have we seen, over the past few months, a significant shift in the political preference of Poland and Hungary, will we see parallel shifts in the West.

If so, there may be a re-focusing on the needs and aspirations of those who have been left behind. Can we begin to identify a new, emerging, pattern?

For those who are trapped in their local community, the likelihood is that domestic living arrangements will be cramped, with little private space for self-actualisation, and a form of public provision which is designed for everybody, and therefore for nobody.

I envisage a substantial demand for designed community spaces which allow people at the neighbourhood level to explore leisure and development activities which are not possible at home. In Europe we have many models on which to draw, but these have not been brought together into an appropriate guidance document **and this I see as an urgent need in the current climate**.

Community libraries, audio-visual centres, display spaces and performance areas are essential for all age-groups, but most notably for the teenager and the old, both of whom have little expenditure for private facilities. Within the continent we have a stimulating series of examples - from socialist central Europe, from Iberia and from the arts centre movement, and we urgently need to update building specifications, and the programmes for community management of such structures. In this, the naively identified, "developing", cultures of southern Europe have much to teach us, especially with regard to democratic management and flexible design.

But we cannot limit ourselves to the structures, for many activities are extended into, or initiated in public space. There is seldom any question as to the availability of such space - traditional areas for performance and parade persists. But it is the management terms under which such activities are permitted which provides the major issue today.

We have to recognise the fact that design, as such, plays a very small part in the effectiveness of either buildings or space for the plethora of cultural activities which may be generated in the local neighbourhood. Much more significant are matters of booking, traffic management, rites, roles and functions which are managed by the municipal authority. Evidently, the local authority can either facilitate local activity, or stunt it through the application of dated regulations or procedures.

6. Making things happen in the neighbourhood

A brief sequence of points separates the neighbourhood which is able to activate its community culture, from that which becomes disillusioned and inward looking. These include:

▶ Recognition: support from the metropolitan authority, elected members and the media.

▶ Financial Resources: to encourage development and public activity.

▶ Stimulus of a Democratic Forum: to encourage public debate, between generation and interests, of the potential for local cultural life.

▶ Promotion: access to media and media skills to promote and validate neighbourhood activities.

▶ Investment: product of performance or activity fed back into the broad context of community culture.

▶ Access to facilities: seldom new build, but an eased path to buildings and spaces for practice, performance and extra-domestic sharing.

Buildings represent a one-off, capital expenditure, which can be cited in the local political debate as a major contribution to local culture. It is, however, a promotional gambit from the authority, rather than for the community. What the community usually needs is the enduring support which only revenue expenditure provides.

This conflict between capital and revenue expenditure is at the root of municipal support for neighbourhood cultural life.

V Public Spaces and City Regeneration

by Giandomenico Amendola
Department of Urban Sociology, School of Architecture
of the Polytechnic of Bari (Italy)

Second Project Conference on
"Urban Regeneration in European Neighbourhoods"
(Bilbao, Spain, 16 - 19 June 1994)

Only fifteen or twenty years ago there was much talk about the imminent eclipse of the city; many were ready to bet on its almost immediate death, and even many academics claimed that urban civilisation - as we have known it - was coming to an end.

The forecast focused not only on geographical or demographic factors but, in fact, mainly on sociological and cultural ones. The city itself, the very heart of contemporary society, would be eclipsed. The focus of the new cultural and geographical system was thought to be the metropolitan region and its communications networks. The landscape of impending post urban society was thought to blend well-connected medium-sized cities with a highly populated rural-urban continuum.

In a world where there is nothing but urban life, these theories claimed that the city would lose its *raison d'être*. It was claimed that modern civilisation can do without the city; people can easily find substitutes and surrogates for urban services, facilities, cultural opportunities and personal experiences elsewhere.

Viable signals of this major event were assumed to be the inversion of a centuries old urbanisation trend, a regional diffusion of traditional city functions, the growing desire of city inhabitants to live in the suburban country or in small towns.

Proponents of this theory agreed that on the one hand inhabitants are pushed out of the city by a long list of urban pathologies and the often unbearable ugliness of urban experiences, and on the other hand, they also argued that people there are drawn out of the city by the possibility of access to some traditional urban functions (eg work, shopping, leisure, services) without leaving home thanks to electronic highways. High-technology makes mass escape from the city feasible. In the electronic or virtual city, even chatting, personal interaction and cultural and political experiences are possible with a computer and a low-priced modem.

The prophecy was that the electronic city would free its people from spatial bounds; in the near future, space itself would become an empty concept. Market, office, school, library, street corner, café and agora could become virtual, non-spatial sites, whose access and use are possible via computer.

But... today and presumably in the near future, the real world fails to match the prophecy. Despite all the pessimistic forecasting (based on demographic or high-tech trends) regarding the decline of the city or its death, the city is still alive. More than ever, the city is central in people's daily lives, in their conscience, in their dreams. There is a growing presence of the city and its light in cultural imagination.

American and European cities are experiencing a new Renaissance, an urban Renaissance. A sign of this new urban wave is a dramatic growth in the use of the city. People move or commute to the city not only to work or to dwell, but also simply to enjoy city life and city mood (Stadtluft). Even shopping can be seen as an urban adventure.

The most important and meaningful indicator of the renaissance of the city is the presence of a social and political demand for the city: people demand "city", they express their right to the city. What is different from the past (the *Droit à la ville* à la Lefebvre) is the content of this urban demand. People want the city and ask for it. What they ask for is not only a list of city functions or facilities, as was the case in the fifties and sixties, but the city itself. What people are explicitly longing for is an enlivened and animated city. A better and more liveable, more beautiful and more accessible urban space.

The content of the demand is a city of lights, a city of variety and encounters, a city with meaningful places, a city that allows people to meet people. What is dying, at least in our conscience, is a city of dead spaces with no sense of place (Stein's: *there is no there there)*; a city made only of functions, a privatised city made of the bare and simple sum of its houses; a city whose only public dimension is the market - a virtual market place with no meaningful interpersonal interactions - a city where the local dimension is evaporating or, if it exists, takes the regressive and residual form of a traditional village.

What people are reclaiming is the public city of the classical European tradition. What contemporary planners, designers, administrators, etc. are trying to create or to regenerate is this public and shining city.

An indicator of this social demand, that often takes a political form, is the growing effort of professionals and administrators to demand, to plan, to build and to manage a better and a more liveable city.

In the last ten years we have been witnessing a tremendous striving to improve our cities. We have been trying not only to improve transport and school systems, housing and roads, but to beautify the city and improve its image, to boost the city's ability to appeal to people and to provide enjoyment.

A keyword in this demand is "public". The social demand for the city, not as a sum of functions and parts, is in its core a demand for that public dimension of urban experience that counteracts the privatisation process. We might say, the original and classical Greek meaning of the word *idiot* - an entirely private person halved by lack of public dimension - has been rediscovered.

In this second urban Renaissance, the practical and symbolic centres of the city are represented by public spaces.

In the last quarter of this century we have witnessed a tremendous increase of public spaces as a major means of revitalising the city and regenerating the public realm.

Since the 1960s, the country which has made the greatest efforts to create or recreate urban public spaces has been the United States.

US planners who advocated the need for urban public spaces have been called "eurourbanists" after the European models that inspired them. Most of the plazas designed in the USA over the last two decades come, explicitly, from the European concept of the piazza. Their name (plazas, not squares), form and details have been chosen to recreate and/or to recall a specific historical experience in which people and built urban form were coherent and integrated.

Plazas, shopping malls, atria, pedestrian malls, festival marketplaces, gardens and parks: a great variety of public spaces have been created in existing city fabric. Old industrial waterfronts, dismissed plants, military facilities, empty spaces in the steel, glass and concrete jungle of central business districts, sidewalks and skyscraper lobbies have been transformed into public spaces. Some of these spaces became places thanks to shops and boutiques, others thanks to concerts and entertainment, others thanks to gardens and scenery, others thanks to their history and architectural heritage. All of these became places thanks to people's use and their desire to meet and to live the city.

Cityscapes changed dramatically in these circumstances. People crowding downtown and in historical areas, in old skid rows and in dismissed docks or industrial areas, nostalgia oriented neighbourhoods are themselves an impressive and appealing urban mobile architecture. A main landmark in contemporary city centres are city users themselves; they are the actors and the stage at the same time.

Until the end of the sixties, most European urban planning and design strategies were aimed at providing facilities, infrastructures, private spaces. Now, European cities are going through the same phase, emphasising and reconstructing public space as a major means of regenerating themselves.

Actions aimed to upgrade old shopping streets, to revitalise historical areas with traditional European approaches have been merging with the American brand new experience of festival marketplaces and downtown shopping malls.

In Europe there has been a greater awareness that a major factor of urban crisis and the desertification of public urban spaces is the crisis of the public man and the weakening of public dimension (öffentlichkeit) of city life.

The existence of an urban public life capable of animating public spaces is not to be taken for granted. (Latin root of animated is anima, meaning soul).

That is why in European strategies the role of public actors is more important than in the USA in defining and implementing public policies - eg cultural policies - able to integrate and balance developers' actions and designers' projects in making public spaces alive and meaningful.

A major issue has been raised regarding the relationship between *agora* and marketplace in the actions aimed to regenerate the public dimension of the city with the creation of public spaces.

Many people argue against the compatibility of trade and cultural activities in public places, the co-existence of the exchange of goods and commodities with transactions of ideas.

On the one hand there is a utopian approach - the hope of recreating Pericles' polis and its agora - on the other hand many planners and administrators advocate the "social realism" of accepting shopping malls or festival marketplaces as the principal modern form of *agora*.

They assume that today's consumer is the contemporary, updated version of the *cives*.

History offers contradictory evidence on this point. Merchants were not allowed in the Greek agora because trade could disturb political and cultural interactions among citizens. And yet most of the piazzas that have been used as models for a multitude of north American plazas were built in mediaeval Italian cities when they were ruled by merchants (the Medicis themselves were merchants and businessmen) and were designed to host the marketplace. Trade was not taken then, as contradictory to beauty: the merchants who governed Siena issued very rigid rules defining the style, windows and form of the buildings surrounding the Piazza del Campo. The built stage of the marketplace was intended to be beautiful.

A similar mix can be found in the contemporary city, where you can visit an art exhibition or listen to chamber music in a Bloomingdales department store or buy furniture and gadgets - even in special or end-of-the-season sales - at MoMa in New York City.

What is new is the change that has now occurred in shopping. People do not go to Covent Garden in London, Quincy Market in Boston, South Street Seaport in New York, to buy; they go in order to enjoy the atmosphere of the places. The contemporary city user is a blend of consumer, spectator and Baudelaireian *flaneur*.

Urban crowds - the so-called *urban tribes* - have different attitudes towards space and different ways of using the city. People can enjoy the same space for different reasons (shopping, meeting, listening, walking, communicating, etc.).

Variety of people and intentions (of both designers and users) is not a problem in creating public spaces: on the contrary, variety is the strength itself of the public places and its main factor of attraction. The same space can and must perform as a stage, a market, a festival place, a recreational area, a simple going-through area, a national heritage or educational site. Public places make urban variety possible.

The underlying intentions of designers and administrators are different: public spaces have been created as the lungs of the city, recreational areas, money producing areas (shopping places), leisure areas, symbolic and identity-building areas. Whatever the intentions, all these areas have given city people the chance to gather and to experience relationships with other people and the city itself.

Places live their own lives regardless of designers' intentions and their first and basic destination. A shopping area and a festival marketplace can become - as they often do - modern *agora* where people go to gather and to enjoy the city mood.

The ability of this generation of public spaces to change in order to meet people's demands and desires while keeping their original destination (shopping, etc) is one of the viable indicators of the success of this strategy of urban regeneration. Other positive signals are the heavy use of the new public places, citizens' ongoing demand for these spaces (the more plazas, etc. are built the more they are requested) and the major role they play in forming a better image of the city. Public spaces, both the new and the revitalised old ones, are becoming a familiar landmark in the daily cityscape.

Public places are created as a means to facilitate the necessary balance between local and global dimensions in urban experience.

Plazas, squares and festival marketplaces are built not only for a neighbourhood or a single community but for all the city and its people. Today, public space is no longer wanted as a setting and a means to hold together the old urban village. Public spaces in their different forms are intended to be freely chosen settings, city spaces able to attract all the city's people.
They act as a link between local and global society and culture and as a means of integrating the city and its parts.

The simple existence of a square does not mean the coming into existence of a public space and the beginning of a new way of experiencing city. The built environment by itself is only a virtuality, a potential space. It is necessary to make it effective and alive.

People are the very creators of space; only people can change projects and spaces into places. Where Boston people turned Quincy Market into a public place, Parisians made the Centre Pompidou and its square an enlivened agora.

Important tools that can help people to create public places - not as surrogates for them - are cultural policies. Cultural life, that is public by its very nature, can endow contents and life to new and old urban public spaces with context and meaning. Culture gives soul to the city.

VI Cultural Considerations in Inner City Regeneration

by Franco Bianchini

Cultural Planning Research Unit, School of Arts and Humanities,
De Montfort University (Leicester, United Kingdom)

Second Project Conference on
"Urban Regeneration in European Neighbourhoods"
(Bilbao, Spain, 16 - 19 June 1994)

1. Introduction

This paper examines the main features of the development of urban cultural policies in Western Europe - with particular reference to neighbourhoods - since the late 1940s. It then discusses in greater detail the uses of cultural policies within regeneration strategies in urban Europe in the 1980s, and the main strategic dilemmas arising from the experience of policy-making in this field in the last fifteen years. Lastly, it identifies a range of debates which are of interest to cultural policy-makers today. Such debates include those about the need to adopt wider definitions of "culture" in policy-making, as well as about the notion of "cultural planning", the social impact of cultural projects and policies, and the potential of neighbourhood-oriented cultural policies.

2. The diversity of the European experience of urban cultural policy-making

One should be careful when generalising about the evolution of urban cultural policies in Western Europe because of the scarcity of comparative research in this area and the great diversity in the definitions of "culture" adopted by city governments. Moreover, interventions by city governments in the cultural field are affected by a number of other factors, whose importance varies in different national contexts. These variables include: the ideologies of political parties in power locally and nationally; levels of local political and fiscal autonomy; the commitment of investors to cities; the configuration of the geography of national cultural economies; the size and nature of local markets for cultural activity, and the influence of external models of policy-making.

3. Cultural policy, urban planning and the role of the neighbourhoods: some common trends

Despite national variations, it is nevertheless possible to outline a common trajectory in the evolution of West European urban cultural policies, and of their relationship with wider urban planning strategies, from the end of the Second World War to the late 1980s. There are important differences in terms of periodisation between different countries and it is, once again, difficult and possibly dangerous to generalise. However, three broad phases can be identified in such a trajectory: from the late 1940s to the late 1960s; the 1970s and early '80s, and from the mid-'80s to the early '90s.

3.1 The age of reconstruction: from the late 1940s to the late 1960s

During the first of the three phases, urban cultural policies were primarily focused on creating or expanding an infrastructure of traditional arts, building-based institutions located in city centres, such as opera houses, museums, and civic theatres, and on widening access to them through the provision of public subsidy. Little attention was paid to the neighbourhoods during this phase. This type of cultural policies was generally accompanied by a top-down, functionalist approach to urban planning, characterised by zoning, greater attention to the needs of motorists rather than to those of pedestrians, the priority of rapidly providing mass housing at affordable costs, and austere, orthogonal Modernist architecture making much use of concrete, glass and steel.

3.2   The age of participation: the 1970s and early 1980s

The development of cultural policies in European cities was encouraged by the decentralisation of powers from central to regional and local government, particularly in Italy in the 1970s, and in Spain and France in the early '80s. Another important factor was the post-1968 emergence of grassroots and social movements such as feminism, community action, environmentalism, youth revolts, gay and ethnic minority activism. These movements were critical of postwar functionalist city planning, and were often closely associated with "alternative" cultural production and distribution circuits comprising experimental theatre groups, rock bands, independent film-makers and cinemas, free radio stations, free festivals, recording studios, independent record labels, small publishing houses, radical bookshops, newspaper and magazines, and visual arts exhibitions in non-traditional venues. This cultural universe challenged traditional distinctions between "high" and "low" cultural forms - for example, between classical and popular music - and adopted a very broad definition of "culture" combining in imaginative ways old and new, highbrow and lowbrow elements. The new urban social movements influenced many local politicians, most of whom belonged to Left parties, who expanded the remit of their interventions to include popular and commercial forms of culture, and recognised that cultural policy could act as a vehicle for social and political change. This new breed of local politicians radicalised the traditional welfarist objective of widening access to city centre-based traditional arts institutions and activities. They promoted individual and group self-expression - and grassroots, community-based cultural participation - also through the decentralisation of cultural provision. Neighbourhood-based activities began to feature in urban cultural policies, often as the result of the politicians' drive to reach social groups which went beyond the traditional audience for arts policies, and of pressure from artistic/political movements encompassing theorists and practitioners, such as "community arts" and "ethnic arts" in Britain, "socio-culture" in Germany and "socio-cultural animation" in France. German cities like Hamburg, for example, developed and implemented educational and participatory programmes for "urban district culture" (UDC) which ranged from political meetings to language classes, music workshops, pottery and research on the history of the neighbourhood.

These cultural decentralisation initiatives were usually accompanied by policies aimed at asserting the role of city centres as catalysts for public life, sociability and civic identity. This strand of policy-making was developed in response to growing social differentiation and inequalities within cities, and to the increasing domesticisation of cultural consumption. It also involved rediscovering and celebrating, as a reaction against the negative effects of functional zoning in land use planning, organic features of cities like density, "walkability", and the overlapping of social, cultural and economic uses. Cultural policies were especially successful in this when combined with urban design strategies to create more public spaces and make the city more attractive and "legible", pedestrianisation and traffic calming measures, and improvements in lighting and public transport. Arts festivals and other forms of cultural animation were used to encourage participation in the city centre's public life for people of different ages, social classes, genders, lifestyles, and ethnic origins. Cultural animation initiatives were also used to give life and meaning back to the "dead" time of the elderly and the unemployed, and to "dead" space, such as industrial buildings made redundant by economic change.

3.3 The age of "urban regeneration": from the mid-1980s to the early 1990s

From the early 1980s there was a clear shift away from the socio-political concerns prevailing during the 1970s, and towards economic development and urban regeneration priorities. A shift to the right in the political climate in most West European countries and growing pressures on the financial resources of local government helped downgrade the earlier emphasis on the importance of access to culture, particularly for disadvantaged groups, and on the decentralisation of cultural provision to the neighbourhoods.

The pressure by national governments on city governments to reduce expenditure initially produced <u>defensive</u> strategies, aimed at preserving existing levels of cultural provision, often by encouraging private sector support for events and activities, and by improving the administration, management, marketing and delivery of services. Later, however, many city politicians and policy-makers began to realise that the process of urban economic restructuring of the early and late 1970s provided opportunities to forge more positive arguments for expanding cultural expenditure. The 1970s emphasis on personal and community development, participation, egalitarianism, neighbourhood decentralisation, the democratisation of urban space and the revitalisation of public social life was gradually replaced by arguments highlighting cultural policy's potential contribution to urban economic and physical regeneration. The language of "subsidy" was gradually replaced by the language of "investment", and new <u>economic</u> justifications for cultural policy-making emerged in many cities. City decision-makers saw cultural policy as a valuable tool in diversifying the local economic base and achieving greater social cohesion. They intervened in expanding economic sectors like leisure, tourism, the media and other "cultural industries" including fashion and design, in an attempt to compensate for jobs lost in traditional industrial and services sectors. A lively, cosmopolitan cultural life was increasingly seen as a crucial ingredient of city marketing and internationalisation strategies, designed to attract mobile international capital and specialised personnel. Participation in cultural activities was promoted also as a way of integrating unemployed young people, new residents, immigrants and social groups displaced by economic restructuring into the local community.

The focus of cultural policy-making shifted once again to city centres, which were seen as showcases for the local economy in the emerging inter-urban competition game, and as engines for economic growth. Peripheral neighbourhoods tended to suffer from the re-orientation towards city centres of the bulk of the resources available for the provision of cultural services. In some cases they also suffered because city governments, in order to finance city centre-based cultural flagship projects, cut expenditure on neighbourhood-based schools, libraries, housing, transport and other services.

4. The impacts of cultural policy as an urban regeneration strategy

The direct impact of urban cultural policies on the creation of wealth and employment in the period from the mid-'80s to the early '90s was relatively small. The main contribution of cultural policies to urban regeneration was in the construction of urban images able to attract visitors. As a complementary factor in the competition between cities possessing similar advantages, cultural policies were also important to appeal to investors and skilled personnel.

Prestigious cultural projects acted as symbols of rebirth, renewed confidence and dynamism in cities like Glasgow, Bradford, Sheffield and Rotterdam, which had been severely hit by the decline of manufacturing industry during the recessions of the 1970s and early 1980s. The city centre of Glasgow benefitted substantially from environmental improvements, the opening of the Burrell Collection in 1983, and the organisation of a lively annual programme of cultural festivals, culminating in the varied programme of events for the "European City of Culture" year in 1990.

In Bradford, the city marketing campaigns co-ordinated by the city council's Economic Development Unit, known as "the Mythbreakers", were crucial for the success of a strategy linking tourism policies with cultural flagship projects. The most important of these was the National Museum of Film, Photography and Television, opened in a converted, redundant theatre building in 1983. The museum attracted 3 million visitors in its first 5 years of existence (Hunter, 1988) and contributed to improving the overall appeal of Bradford as a tourist destination.

Sheffield City Council in 1983, in response to the rapid decline of the local steel industry, started developing in the southern section of its city centre a "Cultural Industries Quarter", focused on the film and popular music industries.

Rotterdam, lastly, similarly improved its image, traditionally that of a dull industrial centre dominated by petrochemical works and the port, through cultural initiatives, including the organisation of new jazz and film festivals and the development of a cultural district in the area around its main museum for contemporary art, the Boymans-Van Beuningen, and the new National Institute for Architecture.

Wealthier cities like Frankfurt used cultural policies to consolidate their competitive advantages, by filling the gap between their high economic status and their relatively low cultural standing. Cultural spending in Frankfurt increased from 6% of total municipal expenditure in 1970 to 11% in 1990. In the 1980s, about 1 billion DM was invested in high quality cultural buildings, converting a derelict opera house into a concert hall and creating a new Museums Quarter on the banks of the River Main.

Dynamic architectural, telecommunication and festivals policies were used as symbols of modernity and innovation in cities like Montpellier, Nîmes, Grenoble, Rennes, Hamburg, Cologne, Barcelona and Bologna, to help develop sectors of the economy such as high tech industry and design-based manufacturing, which depend for their success on cultural inputs. Montpellier, for example, invested heavily in architectural projects, and launched festivals of music, dance, photography, video and cinema. These initiatives were combined with an aggressive city marketing campaign to appeal to mover firms and skilled personnel to locate and work in four technology parks in the fields of agro-industry, pharmaceuticals, computing, robotics and artificial intelligence.

Cultural "flagship projects" like the Burrell Collection in Glasgow, the Albert Dock in Liverpool, Centenary Square in Birmingham, the Antigone district in Montpellier, and the extensive system of new public squares and urban parks - punctuated by sculptures, mosaics and other artworks - created in Barcelona in the build-up to the 1992 Olympics all became powerful physical symbols of urban renaissance.

5. Strategic dilemmas in cultural policy-led urban regeneration

The use of cultural policy in urban regeneration is increasingly an uncontested issue. Yet this consensus masks serious dilemmas regarding strategic choices in economic, cultural and community development. For example, conflicts can arise between cultural provision in the city centre and in peripheral neighbourhoods, between consumption-oriented strategies and support for local cultural production, and between investment in buildings and expenditure on events and activities.

Economic inequities have clear spatial manifestations in many major European cities. New conflicts emerged in the '80s between affluent city centre and suburban residents, and low income citizens living in run-down inner city areas and outer housing estates, whose opportunities for participation in the city centre's cultural renaissance were undermined by a number of factors. These social groups were the main victims of the growth in long-term unemployment and of the deskilling process related to economic restructuring. Rising fear of crime, and the rapid escalation in the cost of out-of home leisure compared with its domestic equivalents contributed to reducing participation by low income groups in more "public" forms of cultural activities. These problems applied even to those cities which had most imaginatively and successfully used cultural policy as a strategy for urban regeneration. The quality of life of the residents in the Glasgow's peripheral and severely deprived housing estates of Pollok, Drumchapel, Easterhouse and Castlemilk, for example, continued to deteriorate at the same time as the city centre was being regenerated and revitalised through a variety of cultural initiatives. This fuelled frustration with, and instances of protest against, the 1990 "European City of Culture" celebrations, by groups such as "Workers' City".

How can the growing divide between lively, convivial city centres in which cultural activities are flourishing and increasingly marginalised peripheries be bridged? One way is by creating neighbourhood-based arts facilities, as demonstrated by the experiences of Hamburg and Bologna. The city state of Hamburg established a system of neighbourhood cultural centres which are used by about half a million people every year for activities ranging from language classes to rock concerts and political meetings. In Bologna, the City Council's "Youth Programme", launched in 1981, re-equipped and renovated the city's neighbourhood youth centres, and stimulated - with the provision of training courses, loans, premises and technical facilities - the flourishing of enterprises in electronic music, video, computer graphics, crafts and other cultural sectors. The new youth centres helped reintegrate many young people into the local economy and civil society.

The establishment of neighbourhood-based cultural centres and the support given to grassroots activities can be successfully combined with the widening of access to city centre-based cultural provision. Accessibility can be enhanced through the introduction of "town cards" to enable local residents to use cultural facilities at discount prices, the wider distribution of accurate information about activities and events, as well as better policing, street lighting, late night public transport and car park safety.

A second type of spatial dilemma in urban cultural policy-making is the need to respond to the fact that, as one graffiti in Montreal proclaimed, in many cases "artists are the storm-troopers of gentrification" (Toronto Arts Council, 1988). The establishment of certain areas of cities as "cultural districts" in some cases - as in Frankfurt's new Museum Quarter (Simor, 1988) - has generated gentrification, displaced local residents and facilities, and increased land values, rents, and the local cost of living, as measured - for example - by the prices charged by local shops. These processes can drive out of the district artists and other cultural producers who survive on relatively low incomes. Such cases clearly demonstrate the limits of unrestrained property-led regeneration strategies.

In the cultural policies of many cities there was a clear separation, which can generate tensions and conflicts, between consumption and production-oriented strategies. The first develop and promote urban cultural attractions and activities as magnets for tourism, retaling, hotel and catering. The second provide strategic support for publishing, film, TV, electronic music, design, fashion and other cultural industries which require specialised skills and infrastructures.

It can be risky in the long-term for cities to rely on consumption-oriented models, even if they may be profitable in the short term, by creating visibility and political returns. The success of consumption-oriented strategies often depends on factors over which cities have very limited control, ranging from airfare prices to changes in the level of the residents' and visitors' disposable income. A related problem concerns the quality of the jobs generated by this type of cultural policies, which are frequently low-paid, part-time, and characterised by deskilling and poor levels of employee satisfaction, legal rights and working conditions. It is therefore important for cities to combine consumption-oriented policies with local cultural industries strategies, which have the potential of creating skilled jobs in high value-added sectors of the economy. Another contentious issue concerns the extent to which cultural policy-makers must choose between "ephemeral" programmes of events and activities - like festivals and other cultural animation initiatives - and investment in "permanent" facilities such as concert halls, libraries, museums and arts centres. This juxtaposition is in many ways artificial. Apparently "ephemeral" events - the Edinburgh Festival, for example - if coherently organised and repeated, can become "permanent" features of a city's cultural landscape, producing long-term benefits in terms of image, tourism and support for local cultural production.

The "ephemeral-permanent" dichotomy, however, does allow us to focus on the problem that maintenance costs and loan charges on cultural buildings such as museums, art galleries, libraries, concert halls, opera houses and theatres - the overwhelming majority of which are concentrated in city centres - are often so high that they absorb most of the resources available. In times of financial stringency city administrations are more likely to curtail revenue funding for those activities which are seen as "marginal", often aimed at disadvantaged social groups or innovative and experimental in character, than to withdraw money invested in theatres, concert halls and other building-based, traditional arts institutions. In this context, greater use of public and open spaces, temporary structures and buildings combining culture with other types of uses could liberate resources to fund more innovative, decentralised and neighbourhood-based cultural activities and projects.

6. Towards a cultural planning approach?

The recognition of the strategic dilemmas raised by the experience of the last decade should inform the process of urban cultural policy-making in Europe today. In the mid-1980s and early '90s urban cultures were energetically exploited by politicians and policy-makers to enhance the reputation of their cities, contribute to the physical regeneration of city centres, boost tourism and other "sunrise" service industries and soften the social impact of economic restructuring. There is no doubt that the emphasis on the importance of consumption, property assets and image was an important addition to the battery of arguments for urban cultural policy-making. The 1980s perspective, however, is too narrow to provide a sound basis for policy development today. City governments should move towards a more holistic "cultural planning" approach, which puts a cultural perspective centre stage when formulating urban development strategies.

The notion of cultural planning, already widely used in the USA and Australia (Von Eckhardt, 1980; McNulty, 1991; Mercer, 1991), is still relatively uncommon among West European policy-makers. It rests on a very broad, anthropological definition of "culture" as "a way of life", and it integrates the arts into other aspects of local culture. Its field of action ranges from the arts, the media, the crafts, fashion and design to sports, recreation, architecture and townscape, heritage, tourism, eating and entertainment, local history, the characteristics of the city's public realm and social life, its identity and external image. Cultural planning can help urban governments identify the city's cultural resources and think strategically about their applications, in areas as diverse as physical planning, townscape design, tourism, industrial development, retailing, place marketing, community development, education and training.

Policy-makers in West European cities are still not sufficiently aware of the potential of their cultural resources. Aesthetic definitions of "culture" as "art" still tend to prevail, and policies for the arts are rarely co-ordinated with policies on sports, the media and other elements of local culture. The result of this lack of integration is the failure to exploit potential synergies and strategic development opportunities. By its nature cultural planning cuts across the divides between the public, private and voluntary sectors, different institutional concerns, and different professional disciplines. To implement cultural planning strategies, city governments will have to move towards a more corporate approach to policy-making.

The movement towards the development of corporate cultural policies is gaining strength. Birmingham City Council, for example, in 1989 merged the cultural functions of five of its Committees in one new, cross-departmental Arts, Culture and Economy (ACE) Sub-Committee. Before its establishment, the Finance and Management Committee was exclusively responsible for grants to major arts organisations, while festivals and community arts came under Leisure Services, the media industries under Economic Development, public art under Planning and arts education under the Education Committee.

The cultural planning approach also reveals the inadequacy of narrowly-based professional specialisations, which may make it more difficult for cities to capitalise creatively on their cultural resources. At present formal training is basically rooted in the traditions of arts administration for arts policy-makers, of marketing studies for tourism development officers and city marketers, and of land use planning for physical planners. There is a clear need for more broadly-based and shared forms of training, which should provide knowledge of urban and regional economics, history, sociology, politics, geography and planning, as well as of European institutions and of models of urban cultural policy in different European countries. The aim of this type of training would be to create a shared language to enable policy-makers to make imaginative connections between their respective areas of work, thereby producing richer and more effective urban development strategies.

7. Conclusions

Adopting a cultural planning perspective would involve rethinking many of the assumptions upon which the policy-making process was based during the last decade. It would be necessary to rethink what the regenerative potential of cultural policy can be. "Urban regeneration" is a composite concept, encompassing economic, environmental, social, cultural, symbolic and political dimensions. Cultural policies, in order to be truly regenerative, should have a positive impact on all of them. The experience of the 1980s was innovative in the symbolic and economic spheres because it linked cultural policy with the "marketing" of cities and with strategies aimed at expanding tourism and other consumer service industries. Urban economic success today, however, depends on advanced industries and services which make intensive use of high quality "human capital" and specialised skills and knowledge. To maintain an important position within future economic development strategies, policies on culture will have to be linked with policies on education, training, research and development.

The 1980s saw a flourishing of studies on the economic importance of the cultural sector in different cities, and of the direct and indirect economic impacts of cultural activities and policies on employment and wealth creation. This tradition of studies was undoubtedly important to raise the profile of cultural policies and to advocate for increased public and private sector investment in culture. In the 1990s, however, new methodologies and indicators will be needed to measure the impact of cultural policies and activities in terms of quality of life, skills enhancement, economic innovation, educational impact, social cohesion and community development.

Similarly, it is important to recognise that city governments in Europe today could share information, best practice and leading edge thinking about urban cultural policy-making much more. This would be valuable since cities in different European countries have different specialisations. For example, the development of local strategies for the media industries (Wynne *et al.*, 1989; Cornford and Robins, 1990; Barnett, 1991; Bianchini, 1991) and of cultural policies targeted at ethnic and racial minorities (Owusu, 1986; Khan, 1991) is more common in Britain than in other European countries, while French cities have a rich experience in the promotion of innovative architecture and new telecommunication technologies such as telematics and cable (see *Medias Pouvoirs*, 18, 1990, and 22, 1991). Cultural co-operation agreements between cities like that recently signed by the municipalities of Montpellier and Nîmes could also be encouraged by the European Union, the Council of Europe and international networks of cities like Eurocities.

In conclusion, it is important to set any discussion about the problems and potential of neighbourhood-based cultural policies within the context of five underlying trends and debates:

1. The recognition of the relative failure of urban economic development strategies implemented in the 1980s, driven by a focus on consumption, service industries and property-led development. These strategies largely neglected the importance of a well-educated, well-trained, self-confident, innovative, creative, resourceful and self-reliant workforce in laying the foundations for economic success. Now the debate on economic futures is shifting perceptibly towards recognising once again the importance of production and of the quality of "human capital". This provides opportunities to make a strong case for neighbourhood-based cultural policies, especially if their impact on skills enhancement can be made explicit, through rigorous impact studies.

New developments in economic theory could help make a strong case for investment in neighbourhood-based cultural activities and projects. According to Ekins and Hutchison in *Wealth Beyond Measure - Some Lessons from Green Economics* (London, Gaia

Books, 1992), five types of capital are needed for successful wealth creation: ecological, human, social, organisational and manufacturing capital. The authors suggest that this should replace the land-labour-capital model of traditional economics. Cultural activities and projects at neighbourhood level could have a significant role to play in the development of human capital (knowledge, skills, motivation) as well as of social and organisational capital.

2. As suggested earlier, due to economic change, polarisation between different social groups within cities - in terms of income, life chances, and access to power and information - has increased remarkably over the last fifteen years, thereby leading to increased conflicts and tensions. There is growing concern about social inequality, embodied in debates such as those about the emergence of the "two thirds society". If neighbourhood-based cultural policies can contribute to creating social cohesion and can help reconstruct channels for social mobility, they would play a major role in counteracting the fragmentation of our urban fabric.

3. Awareness of the interdependence between economic, social, cultural, environmental and political factors is growing. As a result, the inadequacy of narrow functional specialisations in, and approaches to, public policy-making is becoming more and more apparent, with concepts such as integrated planning gaining currency. Cultural policies at neighbourhood level are perhaps uniquely capable of acting as paradigms to show the interconnectedness of the nature of urban problems, and, therefore, of possible solutions to them.

4. Traditional political parties and ideologies are in crisis. Politicians are less and less trusted. Participation in cultural life at neighbourhood level has perhaps the potential to help rekindle political activity and civic responsibility.

5. Racism and xenophobia appear to be growing in some cities, partly as a result of economic insecurity and of the threat to individual and group identity posed by the process of globalisation of the economy in general, and of the cultural industries in particular. A great strength of cultural activities at neighbourhood level could be their potential to develop inclusive, flexible, intercultural and democratic forms of local identity.

Acknowledgements

This paper is based on the opening and final chapters of *Cultural Policy and Urban Regeneration: the West European Experience*, a book co-edited by Franco Bianchini and Michael Parkinson, published by Manchester University Press in 1993. The book includes case-studies on Bilbao, Bologna, Glasgow, Hamburg, Liverpool, Montpellier, Rennes and Rotterdam.

References

Barnett, Steven (1991), "Selling us short? Cities, culture and economic development", in Fisher and Owen (eds.).

Bianchini, Franco (1991), "Urban cultural policy", *National Arts and Media Strategy Discussion Documents*, 40, London, Arts Council.

Blanchard, Simon (ed.), *The Challenge of Channel Five*, London, British Film Institute.

Boden, Trevor (ed.) (1988), *Cities and City Cultures*, Birmingham, Birmingham Film and Television Festival.

Bodo, Carla (1988), "La spesa culturale deglie enti locali: un'analisi quantitativa", in Salvati and Zannino.

Cornford, James, and Robins, Kevin (1990), "Questions of geography", in Blanchard (ed.).

Cummings, Milton, and Katz, Richard (eds.), *The Patron State. Government and the Arts in Europe, North America and Japan*, Oxford, Oxford University Press.

Feist, Andrew, and Hutchison, Robert (1990), *Cultural Trends in the Eighties*, London, Policy Studies Institute.

Fisher, Mark, and Owen, Ursula (eds.) (1991), *Whose Cities?*, Harmondsworth, Penguin.

Khan, Naseem (1991), "Asian arts", in Fisher and Owen (eds.).

Hunter, Jean (1988), "A national museum in an inner city role", in Boden.

McNulty, Robert (1991), "Cultural planning: a movement for civic progress", in *The Cultural Planning Conference*, cit.

Mercer, Colin (1991), "Brisbane's cultural development strategy: the process, the politics and the products", in *The Cultural Planning Conference*, cit.

Owusu, Kwesi (1986), *The Struggle for Black Arts in Britain*, London, Comedia.

Porter, Robert (ed.) (1980), *The Arts and City Planning*, New York, American Council for the Arts.

Salvati, Mariuccia, and Zannino, Lucia (eds.) (1988), *La cultura degli enti locali (1975-1985)*, Milan, Angeli.

Sargent, Anthony (1991), "Views from a big city", in *National Arts and Media Strategy Discussion Documents*, 16, London, Arts Council.

Simor, Anne (ed.) (1988), *The Role of the Arts in Urban Regeneration*, proceedings of a symposium organised by the America-European Community Association Trust and held at Leeds Castle, Kent, 28-30 October.

Toronto Arts Council (1988), *No Vacancy. A Cultural Facilities Policy for the City of Toronto.*

Von Eckhardt, Wolf (1980), "Synopsis", in Porter (ed.).

Wynne, Derek, *et al.* (eds.) (1989), *The Culture Industry*, Manchester, Greater Manchester Economic Development Ltd. and North West Arts.

VII Journey to the Centre of the Neighbourhood

by Jean Hurstel
La Laiterie - Centre Européen de la Jeune Création
(Strasbourg, France)

First Project Conference on
"The Urban Space and Cultural Policies"
(Munich, Germany, 17 - 19 January 1994)

The journey to the centre of the neighbourhood was decided on at the conclusion of the International Congress of Learned Urban and Sub-urban Societies, which took place in Sirius, in the town of Mun-Cheng.

During the congress, a particularly violent clash took place between Professor Messermann of the Mun-Cheng University, and Professor Whiteness of Fordox University. The former claimed that there was no such thing as a neighbourhood, that the neighbourhood was in fact the Atlantis of urban science. As for neighbourhood culture, in spite of endless research, he had found not the least trace of it, not the slightest atom of culture. For his part, Professor Whiteness claimed that the neighbourhood did indeed exist, and that it had not only a body of buildings but also a soul.

The learned European societies then decided to build a machine capable of calculating whether a soul existed or not, in a hypothetical neighbourhood, of a hypothetical town. The machine was baptised NN, the Neighbourhood Nautilus, in honour of the author of Twenty Thousand Leagues Under the Sea.

The NN had an RR: a resource radar, capable of x-raying any wallet, however fat or slim, to the nearest cent. A QQ, which could record not bird-song, but the intellectual quotient, the IQ of any two-legged half-wit. The QQ was calibrated in university diplomas. The NN also had an LL, or liaison laser, for real-time mapping of the sociogram of all the social relations of social bipeds. Obviously, the NN was fitted with armour-plating, painted white, the colour of the UN, protecting it from baseball bats, .22 rifle shots, riots, theft and fire. The NN crew, apart from Professors Messermann and Whiteness, consisted of sociologists, town planners, and educationists, all experts, all Europeans, all university-educated.

At the eleventh hour, a DD was added to the Nautilus' scientific equipment: a disposable detector. Just as a canary measures the oxygen level in a submarine, the disposable detector recorded, or at least one hoped that it did, the emotional output of our hypothetical neighbourhood. The person chosen to carry out the duties of disposable detector was an unemployed artist.

Report of the voyage of the NN to the centre of the neighbourhood:

Page 1, paragraph 1, Professor Messermann

Beneath us, as far as the eye can see, stretches the urban nebula, conurbation of the agglomeration. Oxygen down, exhaust gas up. The town's atomic nucleus can clearly be seen radiating out from the town centre. In the centre, the original atom, the ancient urbs, historic, touristic. All around, N° 19 atoms for the 19th and N° 20 atoms for the 20th century. N° 19 atoms consist of rectilineal and horizontal mineral crystals, while N° 20 atoms take the form of iron and concrete constructions, tending to the vertical. The further we get from the central atom, the further we penetrate into the primitive atomic soup, the urban chaos where atoms lose their atomic structure. In these indeterminate zones, atomic numbers 19 and 20 can either take on the appearance of suburban villas, or more frequently, can form groups according to the formula TBS^2; T for tower, B for block, S for supermarket. Suddenly, the uniform atomic structure is lit up by a flash of radiation. Believe it or not, we are lucky enough to witness a cultural eruption of the central atom – no, what am I saying, it's not just one eruption, it is hundreds of eruptions per hour, one after the other, of an unbelievably high magnitude. Fascinated, the team rushes to the portholes. An incandescent burst of absolutely brilliant music fills the air, followed by a stream of burning lava from an inspired theatrical first night, overlaid by a sustained fire of incandescent stones, absolutely brilliant exhibitions, while the voice of a soprano hits top C, the resource radar becomes white-hot, and an absolutely brilliant dancer is shot into the sky. The eruptions are fast and furious, in the exhilarating atmosphere of spotlights, and the warmth of the media. Oddly enough however, the cultural lava cools down as soon as it crosses the first of the concentric circles. Never mind the surrounding primeval soup. Out there all is dark, all is silent; outside the town walls there is a cultural desert. These are the arid depths of the deepest desert, arid in terms of its resources, arid in terms of its IQ, which drops to 0; it is all very fine to people a cultural desert with houses, supermarkets and factories, none of this makes it any less desert-like or low. A low social level and a low cultural level go hand in hand. When the level really drops, it's known as a hole. Fascinated, absolutely transported by the central cultural eruption, I steer the Nautilus ever closer to the central cultural eruption of the neighbourhood-free town centre. The closer we are to the centre, the closer we are to thee, Oh culture.

A loud shriek. Professor Messermann has been sucked in by the central cultural vacuum, his body becomes luminous, transparent, he has turned into music, song, painting, and then he is no more than an atom in the atomic town.

Now Professor Whiteness grabs the controls and shouts "Let's go down to street level, otherwise we'll be burnt up in the crater of the central cultural volcano. Let's go down 100 feet". The laser starts to glow with a blueish light, and displays a real-time map with very distinct borders. It's unbelievable: over there, between the motorway and the railway, he could see – "No", he said "I don't believe it" – a neighbourhood. "Let's go down further", he shrieked, feverishly, his eye glued to the resource radar as it dropped down and down. "Let's go down another 100 feet", he shouted into the intercom, as the crew choked and held their noses. From the earth arose a dreadful smell of grilled mutton, mingled with sweat and kitchen smells. Whiteness turned pale, Whiteness turned red and said "Gentlemen, I've just made an unbelievable discovery, which will appear in all the scientific journals tomorrow, a piece of news which will silence my critics. I've just discovered what no scholar, no town planner has ever yet discovered: the neighbourhood is inhabited." And he gritted his teeth and said again "Let's go down 100 feet". The crew put their fingers to their ears. Piercing high notes tore their eardrums, while low notes seemed to hit them in the stomach, and unbearable rhythmic cries threatened their sanity.

They looked at each other aghast. Were they headed for heaven or hell? Would the neighbourhood turn out to be just a village full of friendly natives, or a hellish concentration camp peopled by violent drugged barbarians? Whiteness however was chanting songs of the spirit, rhythm is the spirit of the neighbourhood. "Let's go down another 100 feet". And when they saw, in the mist of the winter twilight, the damp walls of the blocks and towers with their vandalised flower beds, their carparks covered with wrecked cars, they closed their eyes. Whiteness, ecstatic, murmured: "The pure beauty of the neighbourhood. The resource radar has gone black, the QQ indicates 0 diplomas. But the liaison laser has gone into overdrive. I have found the centre of the neighbourhood. It is an intense system of relationships. Quick, let's get back to our university solar system". Suddenly a voice spoke: "No" it said "no, we know nothing yet about the neighbourhood. Let us land". It was the voice of the DD, the disposable detector. None of the educationists, sociologists, or town planners was ready to risk his life in so foolhardy an enterprise as physical contact with the natives. And so, he advanced alone to face the smells, the noises and the furies of the neighbourhood. He alone, the transient artist, would serve as litmus test for the culture of the neighbourhood.

The story of the disposable detector.

I went up into a cave: a staircase, seemingly manmade, led to a landing covered with scribbled images. These must be the ancient graffiti or primitive marks of our ancestors. Four mysterious doors faced me, displaying four hieroglyphics which I managed to decipher. Adesselem, Minkovski, Schmitt, Gomez. So the bipeds knew how to make signs which bore a distant resemblance to our earthly writing. I knocked on the door marked Adesselem.

When he opened the door I saw that the lower part of his face was equipped with a phonatory instrument. Incredible discovery, the tribes of the neighbourhood were able to articulate differentiated sounds. Adesselem articulated very clearly, and wonder of wonders, the sounds had meaning. Adesselem articulated signifiers. Adesselem intoned a slow recitative on the subject of his passion, 13th century Arabic calligraphy, which he practised on the kitchen table. He had one great sorrow however: his son was a punk who won all the breakdance competitions, but had failed to get a job in the post office, and his daughter, a champion surfer, sang in the Polish choir. Then there was Minkowski, his neighbour, who showed me the black virgin of Cestokova, who wept tears in the form of dollars, whereas all he could manage were tears of vodka. He was anti-clerical and anti-communist, worked in a furniture factory banging nails into boxes, but in the winter went ice skating on frozen lakes which reminded him of Poland. Whereas Schmitt sang "die Gedanken sind frei" in German. Unemployed, his right to benefits at an end, he came from a family of mathematicians, and showed me his sculpture – his most beautiful creation – "the planetary system according to Kepler: the ellipse", he said, "the ellipse, not the circle, that is the fundamental revelation". Whereas Gomez told me about the war in Spain. He had an orchard in which each tree was named after a comrade killed in the battle of the Ebro. "No passaremos", he chanted, as his daughter flitted in and then out again. She had married a Sicilian who sang old songs about the adventures of Salvatore Giuliano. Five hours, with accordion, tambourine and Jew's harp, while his son had recorded his first digital CD, "Heavy Metal", she said. "The Rebel Sorcerers", that was the name of the group, and they rehearsed in the cellars, inspired by the "Négresses Vertes", yes she hummed:

"The deadly sun,
the deadly awakening,
of the unemployed rebel".

I am caught up in the chaotic and ever-changing flow of the life of the neighbourhood. Objectively, to stop myself going under, I note on my interactive compiler:

1. That the natives of the neighbourhood articulate sounds and signifiers, which clash, entwine, and multiply. Could this be a sign of representations, of values, of behaviour and therefore of cultures belonging to the neighbourhood? I hardly dare believe it.

2. That the natives live in a strange space-time. Memories of the past, going back three generations, spill over into the present and cover several different countries. So far I've only explored a landing with four doors. I dare not think what would happen if the whole block was let loose.

3. That the natives indulge in very strange artistic practices, very different from the ones exploding in the city centre. I have not yet met an opera singer. When I ask them where they can practise, where they can ask questions about the past and present in this

world, they look at me in astonishment. The question had never arisen. The social centre was only for pottery, wicker-work and macramé. They didn't fully understand Barthes' philosophical discourse about Feydeau's "Ne te promène pas toute nue". A leaflet they had found in a letter box, inviting them to an inexpensive event in the Cultural Centre, in the town centre. "Oh," they said, "they weren't cultured, they left school too early".

My own opinion is that neither the cultural centres nor the community centres are cultured because they ignore the multiple cultures, the mixed-race, mingled cultures of the thousands of Schmitts, Adesselems, Gomez', and Minkowskis all around them.

Delicate final word. The neighbourhood is a frontier post between the planetary culture and the inward-looking identity. Between the increasing standardisation of ways of life, of waves of pictures and sounds. The same fashionable look, the same fast-food eating habits, the same series on the television, the same music, the same illness (AIDS), from Los Angeles to Moscow, from Stockholm to Rio de Janeiro; and ethnic cleansing and the return to a mythical identity, a mythical past, a mythical religion, a mythical folklore. The neighbourhood is the happy hunting ground of disappearing species: relationships at work, relationships between ethnic groups, relationships between generations, relationships within the family, and of what is re-emerging from the ashes: new ways of life, new forms of community life, of networks, new cultures, new forms of resistance to racism and to xenophobia.

The neighbourhood is a crossing place, and the ferryman is called the artist. The artist does not work in reality, he is not a social worker. The artist does not work in the imaginary, he is neither journalist nor politician. In the chaos of the jungle, he makes the symbolic sign: the word, or language. The word of self and the word of the other, because any word of self is first of all the word of the other, and over and above images such as the neighbourhood as concentration camp or hell, the neighbourhood as village, what prevails is the single word, the single life, which cannot be reduced to a uniform image, to a statistic, to a survey, to an opinion poll, or to a global vision.

The artist ferrying what is multiple and changing is not producing a work of art saleable on the art market and regulated by the media system.

Neither is he a creator made sacred by an élitist art ideology, and still less the promoter of a populist traditional approach. He is a projector: the man with a project, a desire, and a confrontation between self and the other, in singular space and time. In addition to his work of mourning ancient ways of life and thought, and the values of the past, he traces, compares and imagines the delicate and complex paths which could lead to a possible tomorrow.

These delicate cross-paths, these militants of difference, these projectors of the singular plural exist throughout Europe. We bring them together in a network called Suburbs of Europe which meets each year and whose next meeting will take place in Freyming Merlebach (France) on 3, 4 and 5 February 1994. This year's subject will be the fight against xenophobia. Every day we see the traces at local level of what elsewhere is called ethnic cleansing or fundamentalism.

It is urgent, urgent to let the voice of the excluded, of minorities, of the weak and the unemployed be heard. Contempt for the other, for the other poor, for the other race, for the other religion. It is urgent to speak out for difference, to fight for sensitive and symbolic difference. Otherwise, repressed attitudes will return under the all too familiar guise of fascism or of some other bloodier idealism. The neighbourhood is the place above all others, of human dimensions, where for a little longer at least the simple light of artistic adventure can shine before sinking into the complex shadows of destruction.

VIII Urban Dynamics and Cultural Action

by Michel Bassand
Institut de Recherche sur l'Environnement Construit (IREC),
Ecole polytechnique fédérale de Lausanne (EPFL) (Switzerland)

First Project Conference on
"The Urban Space and Cultural Policies"
(Munich, Germany, 17 - 19 January 1994)

1. The defective development of cities

Defective development, albeit to varying degrees, has been a feature of cities throughout the ages, involving social and spatial disparities and inequalities, segregation, pollution, insecurity and so on. Our own era has not escaped this phenomenon. The city is currently going through a period of crisis. The best and the worst exist side by side in contemporary towns and cities and both need to be taken into account.

Processes such as urban growth and decline, the development of suburbs and dormitories and urban rehabilitation, renewal and restoration are leading to radical changes in modern city life. The town is being replaced by the conurbation. Such conurbations vary greatly in terms of size and their socio-economic structure. Some are very large with a clearly defined centre, others remain small, while yet others are highly dispersed over a large area and appear to lack any coherence. This network of conurbations is dominated by the largest among them: the metropolitan areas. This paper will henceforth focus on such metropolises and the very large conurbations. In France the term metropolis is applied to conurbations of more than two hundred thousand inhabitants. Like many other researchers, I prefer to fix the threshold at one million. The world's metropolitan areas form a vast network. They can no longer be considered in isolation. It is this network which needs to be taken into account, since it forms the centre of the world.

Metropolitan areas and conurbations create serious disparities on the territory of a society: they absorb the momentum of society, leaving the rural areas to die.

A large population and area is not the best criterion for defining this urban phenomenon. Nevertheless, it is frequently used in the social sciences and economics, because it has the advantage of ease and simplicity. Given the complexity of real life this is a risky approach and other criteria need to be added. However, before putting forward other criteria it is worth examining two particularly traditional ways in which such urban communities have emerged:

► Metropolitan areas formed by the growth and extension of existing conurbations which, as a result of various factors, reach and then exceed a population of one million. Classical European examples include Paris, London, Milan and Madrid.

► Metropolitan areas which are formed by the interconnection of two or more conurbations, which thereby attain and exceed the one million threshold. This process results in a network of conurbations forming an identifiable whole, while at the same time permitting the component parts to retain a relative degree of identity and autonomy. One particular example is the Dutch Randstad, but others include the Ruhr, the Northern French metropolitan area (Lille-Roubaix-Tourcoing) and the Lake Geneva metropolis (Geneva, Lausanne and Vevey-Montreux).

Apart from size – about a million or more inhabitants – and area, what other criteria can be used to define a metropolis? Five are proposed, all of which are interdependent and linked to population and area. The five must also be considered extremely variable, which means that they do not all apply at the same time and with the same intensity.

1.1   Global centrality

In an increasingly global society, a metropolis may be defined in terms of its central role in the world. This does not imply that all conurbations of more than a million inhabitants are world centres. However, all are equipped – albeit to varying degrees – with airports, telecommunications centres, universities, industries and service undertakings, cultural facilities and so on which tend to be global in scope. This infrastructure generates very specialised economic activities, in such fields as industrial services, communications and research.

1.2   Segregation

Segregation was already a feature of the medieval town. Other specialists speak, not of segregation but of segmentation, fragmentation or social and spatial differentiation, with each unit identified subject to a dual process of attraction and repulsion. Segregation in the metropolis has become both more openly and more subtly marked. More openly in that vast tracts of metropolitan areas are highly segregated; more subtly because this segregation is accompanied by social and spatial differentiation in terms of the built environment, consumer durables and surroundings. Segregation involves socio-economic, political and cultural aspects.

1.3   Managing mobility

Given the size, in terms of population and area, and fragmentation of metropolitan areas, the movement of people and of products such as information, waste, capital and water and energy resources becomes a critical factor. How to organise these different flows is therefore a key issue for large conurbations. It requires a series of technical and geographical networks – transport, sewage, telecommunications and so on – which are increasingly interdependent and which are linked up to the large number of interpersonal and inter-group social networks which form the nerve system of any metropolis.

1.4   Conflict

The heterogeneity of their populations and the wide range of problems, relating to mobility, pollution, segregation and so on, for which there are no solutions make metropolises focuses of conflict. Such conflict is amplified and legitimised by the high value which modern society places on competition.

1.5   Political Institutions

Practically throughout the world, political power in metropolitan areas is fragmented. Moreover, they lack overarching political institutions to enable them to deal with their multiple problems in a democratic fashion. Individuals and institutions, private and public, try as far as possible, and generally in an authoritarian fashion, to resolve their own problems, which often serves to exacerbate the problems of others. Is there an alternative?

2. The defective development of urban neighbourhoods

The division of towns and cities into quarters or neighbourhoods is a basic phenomenon. However, our understanding of what is meant by neighbourhood has altered significantly, although it still entails segregation.

In medieval and traditional towns, the different quarters formed very strong communities. They often corresponded to three important urban groups: the corporation, the parish and the militia. Generally, however, a quarter only corresponded to one of them, and quarters were already very distinctly segregated.

Industrialisation brought changes to neighbourhoods; social segregation was supplemented by functional specialisation of land-use. Nevertheless, local districts remained very significant communities for all the main social groups in industrial towns – manual workers, the middle classes, young people and so on.

The structure of conurbations and metropolises has given rise to a wide variety of districts and neighbourhoods. Some have retained the style and mode of functioning of the old quarters. However, the high level of mobility in these major urban areas means that the district can no longer be the all-embracing community of former times. Certain inhabitants do undoubtedly remain almost entirely rooted in their neighbourhood, especially the most deprived, the younger and the older townspeople. In general, however, people circulate throughout the city. Local districts tend to retain only a specialised, if still important, function linked to daily domestic life.

Since the early 1980s, defective development, in the form of segregation, has led to an increasing and more frequent incidence of tension in nearly all the principal European conurbations. The inherent workings of the housing market, policies relating to land-use management and ethnic and cultural influences in particular have resulted in certain districts being occupied either by those at the bottom of the social ladder, with all the problems – unemployment, poor education, insufficient integration and so on – which this implies, or by recent or not so recent immigrant groups, whose cultural capital differs markedly from that of indigenous social groups. In other words, these districts are the direct fruit of the segregation process, reinforced by social and cultural exclusion.

The location of these "poorer" neighbourhoods within European and other world cities varies widely. In some cases they are situated in old, run-down inner city areas; elsewhere they are on the periphery, in areas which are of relatively recent origin but which are highly dilapidated and lack all sorts of facilities.

Whether they are located centrally or on the periphery, the social and cultural composition and run-down state of these districts and the social exclusion to which their inhabitants are subject turn them into flash points, giving rise to both internal and external conflict. Fights between neighbours, crime and delinquency, open hostility to non-residents, outbreaks of violence within the district and explosions of all sorts in neighbouring areas and the metropolis as a whole are the most frequent consequences of this form of defective urban development. Naturally, drug trafficking and racism, as well as other forms of repression, become grafted on to the process and accentuate the downward spiral of these disadvantaged areas.

Initial analyses of these areas show that their inhabitants do not challenge the social system as such and in its entirety. They wish not to change it but to become an integral part of it. They are fighting, with varying degrees of hopelessness, against their exclusion and for their integration.

Two points need to be made at this juncture. Firstly, it is the youngest inhabitants who lead the fight, since it is they who suffer the most from exclusion and are most conscious of its absurdity. Secondly, despite their high level of deprivation, the people in these areas exhibit undoubted cultural, musical, pictorial, corporal and other forms of expression. What should be the response to such complex problems? The results of urban analyses and experiments undertaken in all four corners of Europe show clearly that the solution involves economic, social, political, town planning and cultural dimensions. Strictly sectoral initiatives are almost bound to fail. It follows that any measures – whether economic, social or cultural – must from the outset take account of the complexity of the situation and attempt to trigger off initiatives in other sectors of urban life. Moreover, research findings strongly suggest that no solutions are possible unless the inhabitants of these areas are motivated to become directly involved in the implementation of policies which concern them.

It must be stressed that the problems of disadvantaged areas cannot simply be solved internally. The entire urban area has to be mobilised. Progress cannot be achieved if only the inhabitants of the areas themselves are expected to change.

3. Cultural action in disadvantaged areas

The defective social and cultural development of certain areas is thrown into relief by the fact that large conurbations and metropolitan areas contain the most prestigious cultural facilities: museums, concert halls, theatres, universities and schools of all sorts. However, such facilities have little impact on most of the urban population, remaining the domain of the most privileged groups. They tend to reinforce segregation. What sort of cultural policy is therefore required?

The crisis affecting poorer neighbourhoods in the 1980s and 1990s has already been the subject of many investigations, proposals and public policies. It appears that:

▸ if the crisis is to be resolved, policies impinging on all aspects of urban life and of the inhabitants of the areas concerned need to be implemented;

▸ these policies must be directed not simply at disadvantaged areas but at the entire conurbation; the crisis affecting disadvantaged areas is an aspect of the way cities function and is even subject to external forces;

► the local inhabitants must be partners in any initiatives.

These three points do not mean that only multidimensional and global policies are worthwhile. This would be a recipe for inaction. However, each specific policy must be thought through not simply in terms of its internal rationale but also in relation to that of the other policies which together make up the total urban situation. In other words, individual policies, for example on housing, should help to trigger other policies or be harmonised with those already in operation, for example in the fields of education, rehabilitation, the economy, migration and culture, so that instead of conflicting with each other their effects become cumulative.

In the context of the neighbourhoods described above, a cultural policy – be it concerned with music, visual representation, the theatre, literature or whatever – must have at least two objectives:

► to offer inhabitants a sense of direction, in other words enable them to form an identity and draw up plans;

► to develop communication between local inhabitants and with those living elsewhere in the city, in other words to foster greater openness.

In addition, a cultural policy worthy of the name should set in train vertical interaction in both directions and ensure that both occur at the same time: what the author – among others – would call "cultural democracy". In other words, professionals in the cultural field – artists, *animateurs*, teachers – must be mobilised, not to impose their own conceptions of art and culture on local inhabitants but to respond to and stimulate the different forms of cultural expression of the area's social groups, particularly the most disadvantaged. As already noted above, these inhabitants have an authentic culture, which needs to be recognised and encouraged.

We are convinced that cultural democracy, practised in the different artistic spheres, is an effective tool for combating the deficiencies of urban development. This is subject to two conditions, however: that the cultural policy is linked to or triggers other policies in favour of disadvantaged areas and their inhabitants and that the policy is aimed at the most deprived groups in these communities.

4. Conclusions

Segregation and social exclusion are rife in the conurbations and metropolitan areas of Europe. Among other things, they lead to the establishment of local neighbourhoods where disadvantaged groups are concentrated. These districts give rise to serious problems which affect the urban area as a whole.

Among the various measures to help resolve these problems, cultural policies can play an important part. What should this involve?

Following a series of cultural projects relating to cities and regions, the Council of Europe has decided to initiate a project on the theme "culture and neighbourhoods". The project would have four tasks:

1. to analyse the causes and consequences of deficiencies in the development of urban neighbourhoods, a complex phenomenon which varies from area to area;

2. to list cultural initiatives on behalf of disadvantaged areas and the identify those which come within the scope of cultural democracy, because they are particularly innovatory;

3. on the basis of the latter, to formulate recommendations for those with political and cultural responsibilities to ensure such initiatives are applied more intensively;

4. to undertake detailed evaluations of those initiatives which are implemented, since this is the only way of correcting the mistakes which are bound to occur.

Bibliography

Métropoles en déséquilibre? Datar, ed. Economica, Paris, 1993.

Banlieue 89, *Lumière de la ville*, Paris, June 1990.

Bassand M., *Culture and Regions of Europe*, Cultural Policy series, Council of Europe (CDCC), 1993.

Commission nationale pour le développement social des quartiers, *Les cités en question*, Plan Construction, Paris, 1986.

Dubet F., Lapeyronnie D., *Les quartiers d'exils*, Seuil, Paris, 1992.

Jacquier C., *Voyage dans dix quartiers européens en crise*, L'Harmattan, Paris, 1991.

Joye D., Huissoud T., Schuler M., Busset T., Richard J-L, Wolff J-P et al, *Le quartier: une unité politique et sociale*, Lausanne, IREC/EPFL, 1992.

Louis P., Prinaz L., *Skinheads, taggers, zulus et co*, La Table ronde, Paris, 1990.

Moriconi-Ebrard F.,*L'urbanisation du monde depuis 1950*, Anthropos-Economica, Paris, 1993.

Rellstab U., *La culture de quartier: la ville revit*, Commission nationale suisse pour l'UNESCO, Berne, 1988.

Revue des annales de la recherche urbaine, "Développement social des quartiers", April 1985.

Revue Esprit, "La France des banlieues", February 1991.

Revue Pour, "Quartiers fragiles et développement urbain", no 125/126, December 1990.

Roncayolo M., *La ville et ses territoires*, Gallimard, Paris, 1990.

IX Culture and Local Activity in an Urban Environment: the Role of the Neighbourhood

by Dominique Joye
Institut de Recherche sur l'Environnement Construit (IREC),
Ecole polytechnique fédérale de Lausanne (EPFL) (Switzerland)

First Project Conference on
"The Urban Space and Cultural Policies"
(Munich, Germany, 17 - 19 January 1994)

---

1. Introduction

While the recent trend seems to be towards mobility, exchanges and internationalisation (Préteceille, 1991), that does not mean to say that local ties have necessarily disappeared, but perhaps that they have taken a different form (Poche, 1985). It is therefore a question of assessing what nowadays constitutes the bond between inhabitants and their environment (Noschis, 1982, 1984).

The fact that political interest seems, from certain points of view, to be shifting towards the national or international sphere does not mean that the local factor has no part in the discussion (Sorensen, 1988). It would be more true to say that the processes taking place at those various levels are mutually dependent. The neighbourhood therefore constitutes a unit intermediate between citizens and the authorities, in which a number of specific activities or cultural events may be envisaged.

We are also in favour of an approach which links the various aspects of town life. It is impossible to mention neighbourhood culture without tackling the themes of spacial segregation, political culture or style of government. This initial assumption will be reverted to with reference to the examples of 3 typical towns. But at the outset, it is essential to establish a clearly defined methodological framework[1].

2. Methodology

Methodological research has been carried out in 6 towns which differ in terms of language, size and the importance of the neighbourhood associations, so that contrasting solutions can be compared[2]. (Joye et al., 1992)

Initially, we attempted to evaluate available data on the structure of housing and of the residential population in order to assess the degree of social and demographical segregation[3]. By dint of this statistical analysis, it is possible to situate the neighbourhood unit or municipality in an overall system, namely the conurbation; this constitutes a first approach to the impact of populations, and their homogeneousness or lack of it, on local life[4].

---

[1] This presentation is taken from an important piece of research, carried out in the context of PNR25 "Town and transport". Three institutes were involved: Institut de géographie de l'Université de Neuchâtel, Büro Z in Zurich and IREC in Lausanne. A full report is available at the IREC (Joye et al., 1992) and a book is in course of preparation.

[2] Readers who are unfamiliar with Switzerland are reminded that Geneva, Lausanne and Bern are considered large towns, with a population of more than 100,000 inhabitants each, and twice the figure for the urban region. Winterthur has fewer than 100,000 inhabitants and comes within the orbit of Zurich, whereas Neuchâtel and La-Chaux-de-Fonds have fewer than 50,000 inhabitants.

[3] For a detailed analysis of relations between minorities, cf in particular De Rudder (1987, 1991).

[4] This work on segregation and links with the environment indirectly refers to conditions conducive to speaking of a homogeneous "local community", rather than of "local collectivities" (Tiévant, 1983). In the former case, there will be a much greater capacity for internal mobilisation (Dubet, 1985; Pour, 1989; Micoud, 1989).

It is not sufficient to describe the differences between towns or neighbourhoods to gain an understanding of how the neighbourhood functions, what goes on in it and to what extent local organisations – formal or informal – are also channels of communication between inhabitants and the authorities. While an analysis of the press conveys an initial impression of urban issues and local events, it is only after lengthy discussions that one can become aware of the variety of protagonists involved in neighbourhood affairs and the advantages accruing from integration into local networks. The significance of this analysis can be summarised as follows: although everyone is aware that disillusionment with traditional political power-play has militated in favour of new movements, how are the latter organised at local level and what are their links with traditional organisations (Cordey, Gfeller & Martin, 1985, Klandermans & Tarrow, 1988)?

Research was therefore carried out on the basis of discussions with the municipal authorities concerned and members of neighbourhood organisations. Fourteen contrasting neighbourhoods were selected, differing in regard to their buildings, social composition, or even their dynamism. Hence it proved possible to ascertain the special features characteristic of the political organisation of neighbourhood life in six towns: a neighbourhood committee, a representative to listen to the views of the neighbourhood, or else a system based on wide-ranging consultation with the inhabitants of the town as a whole.

After listening to the opinion of the institutional protagonists, we turned to the inhabitants: in each of the selected neighbourhoods, 1,000 questionnaires were dropped into letter boxes. If the number of questionnaires returned is an indication of the interest taken by the inhabitants in their neighbourhood, it has to be acknowledged that the results were modest: with three exceptions[5], between 10 and 20% replied: this shows that the response was not nil, but also that a lengthy questionnaire is conducive to social selection. The replies themselves bring us back to a general problem: how is one to assess the links between the inhabitants' attitude to their neighbourhood, their perception of political problems and their personal involvement in action at local level? What are the connections between the various indicators of geographical location or social status, and involvement in associations or informal networks (Gros, 1986, Guye-Bernasconi & Valiquer, 1986)? The questionnaire also makes it possible to test current interest in certain political issues and to assess any changes in value judgments. In other words, this section is conducive to an evaluation of different ways of belonging and their impact at local level.

More specifically, this part of the research was also conducive to ascertaining whether those concerned – and if so, which of them – were aware of the socio-cultural amenities, or whether inhabitants complained of a lack of such facilities. It was also possible to trace the link between large-scale cultural facilities in towns and local activity as perceived by the citizens concerned.

3. From the citizens' point of view

How do citizens, or town-dwellers nowadays perceive their town and neighbourhood and what use do they make of them? How is urban management viewed? What is there in the way of socio-cultural activities? How substantial is political participation in this context and, in the opinion of our respondents, what forms ought it to take? We might test a few hypotheses in the light of those questions.

---

[5] A delivery service was used to distribute the questionnaires in three neighbourhoods, whereas we distributed them ourselves in the others. Only half the number of replies was received from the neighbourhoods covered by this service.

▸ At the present time, particularly as a result of much greater mobility and the dispersal associated with commuting, the feeling of belonging is conditioned much more by one's personal concept of one's environment than by reference to activities confined to limited geographical areas, such as neighbourhoods (Lamarche, 1986; Amphoux et al, 1988).

▸ This means that environmental policies (D'Arcy & Prats, 1985) play an increasingly important role in the context of urban policies, in so far as they may affect the inhabitants' image of their own neighbourhood or the way in which it is perceived by the rest of the town. In that case, the social implications must have become slightly less significant.

▸ Policies to encourage socio-cultural activity are on the borderline between social policy and environmental policy. Depending on the town or neighbourhood in question, stress will be laid on one or other of those aspects. Here the assumption is that towns which are more sensitive to their social climate will provide a closely knit network of infrastructure facilities, whereas towns which are more dependent on local pressures will have recourse to more lightweight forms of socio-cultural activity.

▸ Political affiliations are changing. Alongside the traditional organisations and parties – which, moreover, are frequently linked – a network is being set up to encourage participation in all sorts of movements, susceptible to being mobilised by the most eye-catching local events (Auer & Levy, 1986; Duvanel & Levy, 1984).

Participation is considered in this context to vary, depending on whether it concerns formal or informal organisations (Kellerhals, 1989) and whether it involves conventional political action (elections, referendums) or unconventional political action (demonstrations, boycotts, etc). This can be explained in terms of position in the widest sense, including both social and spacial links, as well as ethical standards and attitudes.

Furthermore, it will also be necessary to establish the importance of the neighbourhood as a frame of reference. It is assumed that its relations with the town in particular, but also how outward or inward looking it is, will have a far-reaching impact on any actions undertaken in it. Accordingly, the neighbourhood is seen as a context for action, which has to be taken into account in any event.

Other data appear to be basic variables, to be used systematically in analysing the replies to the survey, but possibly also in any action undertaken in situ. We shall mention four of them in particular, two relating to **geographical location** and two to **social status**.

1. **Experience of mobility** plays an important role in our theoretical model. On the one hand, if individuals have experienced mobility outside their region of origin, they might have come into contact with other models of political activity and consequently view their commitment in a different light. On the other hand, local integration cannot be the same if people have always lived in their neighbourhood or town as when their lives have consisted of moves and new starts. In the first case, a model reminiscent of a village within a town is still conceivable; in the second case, it is hardly likely. At first sight, the findings suggest that mobility is an explanatory variable: but in fact its effect depends primarily on social status: socio-professional categories with the greatest cultural capital also tend to be more mobile.

2. **Frequented areas and local integration** fall into a somewhat similar category. The question is whether the neighbourhood merely constitutes one place among others, or whether it genuinely represents a relatively important living area. The separation of living and working areas may have an impact on local integration and

involve a change of scale for the individual. One of the main challenges of local management today is to match levels of management, which are generally on an urban scale, to the individual lifestyle, which is more closely linked with tiny areas, and possibly several such areas (Haeberle, 1987; Levy, 1990).

3. **The stage people have reached in their life cycle** is of traditional significance in sociological enquiries. This variable in fact involves two dimensions. On the one hand, it indirectly reflects the age of the person concerned, in so far as most respondents leave the parental home, have children, etc at relatively similar ages. But, on the other, it also has to do with the composition of the household: whether it consists of a single person, a childless couple, a couple with children; whether the latter are still small or, if they are older, whether they are preparing to leave their parents' home. It is primarily the last factor that we have considered here. The findings demonstrate that **the presence of children** is conducive to greater involvement in neighbourhood affairs. There is in fact a powerful link between lifecycle and social integration.

4. **Social status** in the strict sense of the term is obviously the sociological variable par excellence. Even though class barriers seem to be breaking down and even though social class no longer has the significance which could be attributed to it in the past, it seems to us important to consider this dimension as crucial to test carefully its impact of the dependent variables and to consider interactions in the explanatory model. Generally speaking, the survey shows that social status is decisive as regards participation in associations and in traditional politics and the extent to which people are informed about the way the town operates.

Throughout this paper, we have moreover stressed the importance of images and representations. It is quite clear that those which relate to a neighbourhood or town have pride of place. In this context, it is important to ascertain – in the light of our respondents' positions – whether neighbourhoods are characterised primarily by physical features, such as the built environment, or by reference to the population living in them, and whether the residents' assessment corresponds to the dominant characteristic of their neighbourhood, or whether certain social groups are more visible than others.

The findings do not invalidate those hypotheses. It can be said that most of the respondents use the town rather than just the neighbourhood. As Jacques Lévy writes (1989), "A neighbourhood cannot be regarded as a small-scale model of local areas, since a projection of the individual neighbourhoods taken as a whole entirely fills the map of the town centre". Even the urban area proves inadequate on its own: 60% of the respondents have already lived outside the urban centre in which they now reside.

Nor is the contention that images are increasingly important invalidated a priori: the landscape and architecture are mentioned by 30% and 20% respectively as the factors which best distinguish the neighbourhood from the town; 25 and 20% respectively opted for the atmosphere and the inhabitants[6]. Lastly, the question of environmental policies is a very real one, although it is not always possible, in terms of specific examples, to disentangle a genuine political approach from a matter of immediate concern. It is nonetheless true to say that, for example, a third of the respondents considered traffic problems to be disturbing, whereas only 1/8th said the same about the lack of social amenities. Similarly, while generally speaking, the social characteristics of each neighbourhood are clearly recognised and correspond to the image an inhabitant of the particular neighbourhood concerned likes to

---

[6] In commenting on the latter points, we should point out that our opinion poll only provides for an assessment at a given time, whereas in order to validate the hypotheses it would, strictly speaking, be necessary to carry out a series of tests over a specific period.

project, the demographic features, which describe the resident population, are less well known. This latter finding would tend to demonstrate that sociological characteristics are of greater use as frames of reference than the demographic composition of the population, although this latter aspect may also be visible and contribute to a neighbourhood identity.

A lack of activity is generally deplored in all neighbourhoods, though to a much greater extent in the richest ones than in working class neighbourhoods. Similarly, community centres and facilities of this kind are much more visible in areas inhabited by intellectuals or middle class professionals. Lastly, there seems to be acceptance of the financing by public authorities of prestigious cultural facilities in the same way as support for neighbourhood community centres or local cultural facilities.

Those factors would seem a priori to support the hypothesis of a change whereby greater importance is attributed to "post-materialist" values than "materialist" ones. But, in order to prove this, one has again to assume an equivalence between, on the one hand, a "materialist" attitude, defined on the basis of the importance attributed to political themes expressed in terms of "left" and "right" – such as commitment to social policies – and, on the other, a "post-materialist" attitude, characterised by an interest in the ecology of the urban milieu and the importance attributed to environmental policies.

Two findings are particularly interesting in this connection. Firstly, contrary to Inglehart's findings (1990), there is not merely a conflict between the earlier, materialist values which are being abandoned in favour of modern, post-materialist ones that are gradually taking their place, but the two are used jointly to define the issues of urban policy[7].

---

[7] In terms of factor analysis, it is not possible to speak of a two-pole axis as Inglehart proposes, but one has to consider two single-pole axes.

At the same time, it should be noted that, in the respondents' view, the differences between socio-professional categories are defined not so much in "materialist" terms as in terms of "post-materialist" values. This implies that the explanatory factors put forward in the political debate have perhaps shifted, even if the underlying values are still quite coherent. Consequently, it is possible to expect a commitment to both social progress and socio-cultural activity in quite a few neighbourhoods.

To what extent is lengthy experience of a neighbourhood a prerequisite for participation in local affairs, and is such participation more readily formalised after many years of residence? Naturally the concept of participation is a broad one; for example, militancy in political parties, unlike action in local movements, does not necessarily presuppose territorial attachments. In this context, **is social status the decisive factor, or does geographical affiliation play a more important role?** Our findings would tend to lend credence to the contention that social status plays an essential role, whereas geographical location is more likely to determine the rules of the game, depending on whether the town in question has a more or less representative democracy, the degree of institutionalisation of neighbourhood associations etc. Within towns, segregation also plays a part in matters such as traffic control, where individuals tend to defend their territory, with a degree of vehemence directly related to the homogeneousness of the population concerned.

Integration into networks is also a factor which goes to explain why people know about decision-taking processes and know those who participate in them or, on the contrary, why there is among them the feeling of being defeated by the ways in which the town operates. In this case, there are various possibilities: integration into a neighbourhood, into a town as a whole or into a conurbation. One of the issues in our survey is in fact to determine whether the neighbourhood is a sufficiently all-embracing unit for priority to be given to integration at this level or whether – through a network of social facilities – the town or urban centre is not the more meaningful level of reference. This investigation is all the more necessary in view of the fact that there is still lively support for the view, which is regularly aired as soon as mention is made of neighbourhood democracy – that what is small is necessarily closer to the citizens concerned.

This relatively brief review goes to show that the neighbourhood is not an area defined a priori in terms of official boundaries[8]. In actual fact, it is more a framework for action, in which an analysis of urban problems can be reconsidered, from the viewpoint of citizen participation; it is obviously an integral part of the political functioning of the towns under consideration. In this context, two aspects have to be borne in mind.

Firstly, to what extent does the prominence of a problem determine the action, or is militancy – taken in the widest sense of the term – the explanatory factor? In other words, what creative role is played by "spontaneous" movements as compared with more institutionalised action? It is obviously crucial to put this question when socio-cultural facilities are being installed.

We, for our part, would be tempted to maintain that it is scarcely possible to embark on any action unless there is already a minimum of existing structures. However, according to Benoît-Guilbot (1986), galvanising actions are often short-lived and the structural minimum would therefore consist of certain individual relationships which might be incorporated within several networks. Furthermore this latter aspect would help to explain the extent to which situations differ in the various

---

[8] The neighbourhood as defined by its inhabitants is generally smaller than that officially defined. But it should be noted that the more institutionalised the neighbourhoods become in a given town, the greater the area they appear to cover (Joye et al, 1992).

towns under consideration. The information available also lends credence to the hypothesis of a multiplicity of networks: 5% of respondents maintain that they are active members of a party, 7% are sympathisers, but approximately one quarter claim to be members of associations involved in local affairs. They would therefore appear to have recourse to a variety of bodies to defend their interests. However the question of membership of associations raises the question as to who participates, and under what terms. In the latter case, we have just seen the importance of social status. We should also be aware that this question of participation goes hand in hand with this issue of confidence in the authorities, which is minimal in the case of half the respondents. Generally speaking, even if there are a great many networks, including ones for conveying to the authorities any conceivable complaints and requests, there is little interest in traditional politics as a means of participating in local affairs.

Secondly, which urban issues attract the most political involvement; is it in fact environmental policy, or do less spectacular policies with greater long-term effects, such as social policy in particular, play an equally important role? There again, one has to establish whether social status is the explanatory variable in the importance attributed to a specific problem, or whether experience as a resident with practical knowledge of a neighbourhood is, at any given time, an equally powerful factor.

The findings show that the processes are different, depending upon the nature and scale of the problems at issue. Petitions concerning social policy are more usually expressed through institutions, whereas traffic control, for example, is organised at local level, in a much more flexible way. Lastly, the likelihood that an initiative launched by citizens will succeed is also a vital parameter: in practice, if four to five years of effort do not culminate in success, the participants tend to give up and withdraw from collective action, with a residual feeling of bitterness.

Finally, research has so far shown that participants who are relatively well integrated into neighbourhoods, or more or less closely associated with networks acting within a conurbation, are willing to become involved in local policies. One of the essential issues is precisely the linkage between integration into a neighbourhood and wider social commitment, ranging from local activities to social policy. We uphold the contention that this question is closely bound up with urban structure; that is why it is relevant to consider three typical examples.

4. Three towns as typical examples

In an attempt to generalise about the system within which inhabitants go about their daily business, we shall describe what has happened in three Swiss towns. To avoid becoming bogged down in local peculiarities, we intend to call them A, B and C[9]. In each case, we shall attempt to follow the system of segregation used and the policies pursued, beginning with a policy for cultural activity, linking them with associations before demonstrating their impact on local life.

4.1 Town A

The urban region of A is clearly structured, from a territorial point of view: the municipalities are large and they have additional influence owing to the autonomy conceded under cantonal law. Relatively speaking, the same is true of the urban neighbourhoods.

A is an example of an urban region in which political processes are, as it were, localised. Urban projects and problems are attributed to specific areas and any conflicts which may arise are, to the greatest possible extent, reduced to their territorial dimensions. In this way a political

---

[9] These examples, which are slight caricatures, are based on Swiss towns which we actually studied. We leave it up to the inquisitive reader to guess which town corresponds to each model.

consensus has been achieved in an attempt to integrate "all concerned" by proposing a representational model based on the distribution of the political parties. In so far as neighbourhood organisations – the traditional representatives where neighbourhood affairs are concerned – failed to fulfil the prerequisite of representativeness, neighbourhood committees were set up to settle local questions in the town as a whole. In practice, it did not prove possible to set up such committees in all neighbourhoods, if only because of the exacerbation of the conflict between left and right.

Model A has undoubtedly been successful in the field of environmental management: transport problems seem to have been satisfactorily solved, and the public has been involved in devising individual projects. On the other hand the extremely localised approach adopted by policy-makers in Bern has two major disadvantages. A forward-looking approach based on the concept of developing an overall project for the urban region is still in its infancy and it is by no means a foregone conclusion that the rural areas making up the canton as a whole will encourage the capital to develop along those lines. On the other hand, the priority given to local management makes it extremely difficult to solve social problems and integrate a marginal population. The recurring examples of reactions to youth movements, or even the way in which the drug problem is being tackled, are certainly indicative of this.

Any explanation of this system naturally cannot disregard the long-standing political tradition, but it also has to be geared to the social structure of the neighbourhoods. While there is a good deal of segregation in terms of life cycle, there is relatively little of it in terms of social status[10]. Hence relatively similar associations were able to

---

[10]   It should be noted that there is a system of housing support which give priority to personalised assistance rather than subsidising the building of large estates, i.e. council housing, which easily fall into disrepute.

evolve in each of the neighbourhoods and acted as a link between a majority of inhabitants and the authorities. This process was encouraged by the fact that there is both a low proportion of foreigners and relatively little mobility. However, such conditions are fairly exceptional in large Swiss towns.

From a socio-cultural point of view, model A provides support for the claims of those citizens who are best established locally. Self-employed persons with small businesses, who are not very mobile, have powerful networks at their disposal; social categories comprising intellectuals, who are highly mobile, have difficulty in developing their own activities outside the scope of "official culture", whereas the somewhat marginal social categories may rapidly find themselves in conflict with the authorities, in the absence of a niche which they can call their own.

4.2 Town B

In many ways, B's image seems to be completely different from that of A. For instance, the municipal autonomy of the one contrasts with the universal presence of the cantonal administration in the other. Furthermore, for many years this institutional feature favoured the development of the urban region as a whole: an international role, an airport, specialised services, as well as protection of the agricultural area. This overall policy is now being called in question by an extension of the conurbation beyond the cantonal boundaries, or even national ones, necessitating new forms of co-ordination.

For a good many years, B's policy has been distinguished by a willingness to lend an ear to any passing trends, sometimes up to and including the relatively far-flung fringes of a certain milieu: those representing an alternative cultural scene and squatters – to mention just particularly obvious examples – have thus enjoyed a right to recognition[11]. The development of local community centres has to be considered within this very general framework. Consequently, very few problems are initially raised at neighbourhood level, but there is generally considerable willingness to listen. Within the political process, relatively little stress is accordingly laid on the local or localised aspect, but much greater importance is attributed to the protagonists and any alliances they may conclude. New movements thus have a greater impact than traditional associations.

The advantages and disadvantages of such a system once again seem to be a mirror image of A's situation: generally speaking, the social problems seem to have been relatively well solved, whereas less concern has been shown for the environment than elsewhere. The traffic problems have become critical and air pollution, for a town without any heavy industry, has reached alarming levels. Furthermore, blatant differences in the quality of life, associated with a high degree of social segregation, have become apparent as between one neighbourhood and another. Even though high segregation is to some extent curbed by high mobility, it is nonetheless likely to spark off demonstrations of discontent which might prove violent. In this context, the exclusion of the foreign population from political movements could, in the medium or long term, turn out to be a serious mistake.

4.3   The situation in a medium-sized town: C

From several points of view, C is going through a major upheaval, which is reflected in an increasingly large gap between traditional institutional structures and prevailing economic and social conditions. The town, whose image has been profoundly affected by the building of a motorway, is also faced with major financial problems.

---

[11]   Conversely, the lack of socio-cultural activity is criticised in the richest neighbourhood, even though its local community centre is extremely well equipped.

The town and its conurbation are relatively well balanced: even within the urban centre, there is not much difference between one neighbourhood and another. This absence of internal differentials and C's relatively small size have been an impediment to the emergence of specific neighbourhood units. Neighbourhood organisations only exist in two places and are still kept going thanks to the personal initiative of one or two individuals. This type of organisation, which largely relies on voluntary work, has also become the exception in medium sized towns and is likely to disappear entirely. At the same time, direct consultation between the authorities and a growing population is proving less and less effective as a means of settling the day-to day problems.

During the past few years, town C has been trying to establish its relationship with its population on new bases. Subsequent to an initiative taken by the authorities and mobilisation of a large sector of the population, the dominant issue of traffic control has culminated in the setting up of neighbourhood associations virtually throughout the town. It is still too early to assess whether those associations will be able to survive in the long term. In actual fact, traffic control is probably one of the few environmental issues which is of direct interest to the population as a whole. Nevertheless, it is certainly worth building on those first attempts at decentralisation and making them more widespread, if only to prevent the local level from becoming a political no-man's-land.

The question of size is crucial in this context: how can a medium-sized town, with a population scarcely larger than that of a neighbourhood in a capital city, simultaneously provide cultural facilities fulfilling the need to promote the region in general, while – at the inner city level – offering specific facilities which are all the more necessary in view of the fact that an earlier "community" model – ideally including all the inhabitants – undoubtedly seems to belong to the past? In any event, it would seem that there is a maximum size for large-scale schemes in the socio-cultural domain.

5. Conclusions

In conclusion, it should firstly be recalled that our commentary has outlined general trends. If one wishes to gain a better understanding of the political actions taking place in specific neighbourhoods as well as of relations between the inhabitants and their environment, a typology of the inhabitants has to be established: with the help of such an analytical tool, it will be possible to rediscover urban diversity. To cite just one example, if inhabitants are asked to define the areas in which they consider themselves to be citizens, it is very likely that they will mention several levels. That is what we call the superimposition of citizenships. There too, the findings reveal a more frequent reference to large spatial units on the part of respondents from the upper social classes or those with an experience of mobility.

In relation to the inhabitants, the argument runs along similar lines. Certain experiments show that the possibility of expressing oneself in relation to one's environment may constitute a way of becoming integrated into the local political system. It should, however, be noted that neighbourhood movements only operate satisfactorily if there is a sufficiently high likelihood of their being successful: this form of participation has to be able to rely on concrete results. Furthermore, it is impossible to deal with all the problems arising at local level with the same degree of success. In actual fact, environmental questions lend themselves most satisfactorily to such negotiations, possibly to the detriment of social issues.

With regard to urban policies, it is interesting to note that subsequent to an analysis of how the various towns function at local level, it has been possible to update two models. Model A is conducive to a maximum number of problems being dealt with at neighbourhood level. Consequently, local planning questions have been satisfactorily settled, but it is more difficult to bring a project to a successful conclusion when it involves the town as a whole, especially if it has little impact on spatial planning. On the other hand, model B tends to operate more through party political networks involving the town as a whole, which prove effective in connection with social issues, but are less so when a local project has to be defended. These differences of organisation are matched by different criteria governing access: under the first system, many years of residence may seem necessary for people to be able to intervene, whereas the situation is not the same in the second case.

In regard to socio-cultural questions, the degree of commitment differs, of course, depending on whether the neighbourhood genuinely constitutes a point of anchorage, or is simply one place amongst others to be used in the town. In our view, the problem is all the more critical in that it is bound up both with the local socio-political system and with the typology of the inhabitants, in so far as use of the town and its facilities depends not only on social status, but also on the type of relationship with the environment[12].

As far as the authorities are concerned, does the neighbourhood represent a useful level for consultation? Naturally when political communication is functioning inadequately and when confidence in the authorities has been eroded, any level of consultation – including neighbourhood consultation – is valuable. This is all the more true in that frequently it is primarily the form, i.e. the way in which projects which have already been decided on are introduced, which creates a problem rather than the fundamental issue[13]. Furthermore, in such a process, it is undoubtedly vital to have reliable partners, with whom it

---

[12] In other texts, we have expressed this differentiation on the basis of an account of the "conceptual" and the "practical" respectively. Cf in this connection *Amphoux et al (1988)* or *Joye et al (1990)*.

[13] It should be noted that this problem of communication has widely been imputed by our respondents to the authorities, much more so than to politicians, who nowadays are fairly well aware of this need to communicate.

134

is possible to establish long-term relationships based on mutual trust. These arguments in favour of a wide-ranging consultation at neighbourhood level imply criticism of institutionalisation: the more inflexible the procedures, the more the partners agree on the need to defend their immediate environment, and less accessible politics tends to become, thereby excluding those citizens who are least integrated into the local system.

Bibliography

Abélès P. (1991), *Faire la politique, Autrement*, Paris.

Amphoux P., *et al.* (1988), *Mémoire collective et urbanisation*, 2 tomes, Lausanne and Genève, IREC and CREPU.

Auer A., and Levy R. (1986), "Les mouvements de quartier face aux autorités et aux partis", *Annuaire Suisse de Science Politique*, No. 26.

Benoit-Guilbot O. (1986), "Quartiers-dortoirs, quartiers-villages: constitution d'images et enjeux de stratégies localisées", *L'Esprit des Lieux*, Paris, CNRS.

Cordey P., Gfeller P., and Martin J. (1985), "Luttes urbaines à Genève", *Revue Suisse de Sociologie*, Vol. 12, No. 3.

d'Arcy F., and Prats Y. (1985), "Les politiques du cadre de vie", L. Grawitz and J. Leca (eds.), *Traité de Science Politique*, T. 4: *Les Politiques Publiques*, Paris, PUF.

Dansereau F. (1985), "La réanimation urbaine et la reconquête des quartiers anciens par les couches moyennes : tour d'horizon de la littérature nord-américaine", *Sociologie du Travail*, No. 2.

de Rudder V. (1987), *Autochtones et immigrés en quartier populaire*, Paris, CIEMI and l'Harmattan.

de Rudder V. (1991), "La recherche sur la coexistence pluri-ethnique. Bilan, critiques et propositions", *Economie et Société*, No. 64.

Dubet F. (1985), "Développement social des quartiers", *Les Annales de la Recherche Urbaine*, No. 26.

Duvanel L., and Levy R. (1984), *Politique en rases-mottes*, Lausanne, Réalités sociales.

Gaudin J.P. (1989), "Décentralisation et nouvelle citoyenneté locale", *Politix*, No. 7-8.

Gros D. (1986), "Les acteurs des luttes urbaines", *Revue Suisse de Sociologie*, Vol. 12, No. 3.

Guye-Bernasconi M., and Valiquer N. (1986), "Le jeu des classes moyennes dans la mise en scène urbaine", *Revue Suisse de Sociologie*, Vol. 12, No. 3.

Haeberle S. H. (1987), "Neighbourhood identity and citizen participation", *Administration and Society*.

Inglehart R. (1990), *Cultural Shift*, Princeton, Princeton University Press.

Joye D., Leresche J.P., Schuler M., and Bassand M. (1990), *La question locale, un éternel sujet d'avant-garde*, Berne, Conseil Suisse de la Science.

Joye D., *et al.* (1992), *Le quartier, une unité politique et sociale*, Research Report No. 98, Lausanne, IREC.

Kellerhals J. (1989), "Action collective et intégration sociale : éléments pour une typologie de la participation associative", *L'Autosuggestion disait-on !*, Cahiers de l'IUED, Paris, PUF.

Klandermanns B., and Tarrow S. (1988), "Mobilisation into social movements: rynthesizing European and American approaches".

Klandermanns B., Kriesi H., and Tarrow S. (ed.) (1988), *International Social Movement Research, Vol. 1: From Structure to Action: Comparing Social Movement Research Accross Cultures*, Greenwich and London, JAI Press.

Lamarche H. (1986), "Localisation, délocalisation et relocalisation en milieu rural", *L'Esprit des Lieux*, Paris, CNRS.

Lévy J. (1989), "Quel espace pour la démocratie urbaine ?" in C. Gagnon, J.L. Klein, M. Tremblay, *Le local en mouvement*, Chicoutimi, GRIR Université du Québec à Chicoutimi.

Lévy J. (1990), "Espace politique et changement social", *EspacesTemps*, No. 43-44.

Mabileau A., *et al.* (1987), *Les citoyens et la politique locale*, collection vie locale No. 11, Paris, Pedone.

Micoud A. (1989), "Le développement local ou comment construire de nouveaux territoires", *Revue Internationale d'Action Communautaire*, Vol. 22/62.

Noschis K. (1982), "Identité et habitat", *Cahiers Internationaux de Sociologie*, Vol. LXXII.

Noschis K. (1984), *Signification affective du quartier*, Paris, Méridiens Klincksiek.

Poche B. (1985), "Une définition sociologique de la région ?", *Cahiers Internationaux de Sociologie*, Vol. LXXIX.

Pour (1989), *Les régies de quartier*, Paris, l'Harmattan.

Préteceille E. (1991), "Paradoxes politiques des restructurations urbaines. Globalisation de l'économie et localisation du politique", *Espaces et Sociétés*, No. 59.

Russel J.D. (1988), *Citizen politics in western democracies*, New Jersey, Chatham.

Sorensen R. (1988), "Civic action groups in Switzerland: challenge to political parties?", K. Lawson and P.H. Merkl *When parties fail*, Princeton, Princeton University Press.

Tievant S. (1983), "Les études de communauté et la ville : héritage et problèmes", *Sociologie du Travail*, special edition.

Wehrli B. (1987), "Demokratische Mitwirkung an der Raumplanung", *Annuaire Suisse de Science Politique*, No. 27.

X Bibliography on Culture and Neighbourhoods

by Franco Bianchini and Massimo Torrigiani
Department of English, Media and Cultural Studies,
School of Arts and Humanities, De Montfort University
(Leicester, United Kingdom)

This bibliography is meant to provide an initial guide to orientate the reader through the vast literature related to urban neighbourhoods. It comprises texts published over the last two decades, with the exception of materials concerning the definition of "neighbourhood" and related terms, given that some of the "classics" in this field were published before 1974. Texts are grouped under the following categories:

1. Community development
2. Community relations
3. Culture and neighbourhoods
4. Definitions
5. Deprivation
6. Descriptions of neighbourhood life
7. Education
8. Employment and labour market issues
9. Housing
10. Neighbourhood media
11. Neighbourhood politics
12. Neighbourhood regeneration
13. Social networks
14. Social policy
15. Social stratification
16. Sustainability issues
17. Voluntary sector

1. Community development

Baine, S., Benington, J., and Russell, J. (1992), *Changing Europe. Challenges Facing the Voluntary and Community Sectors in the 1990s*, London, NCVO.

Besset, T. (1991), *Associations de quartier traditionnelles à Berne et à Genève. Contribution à une étude de la sociabilité urbaine*, Lausanne, Institut de Recherche sur l'Environnement Construit.

Chanan, G. (1992), *Out of the Shadows. Local Community Action and the European Community*, final report of the research project "Coping with Social and Economic Change at Neighbourhood Level", Luxembourg, Office for Official Publications of the European Communities.

Community Development Foundation (1992), *Arts and Communities*, report of the National Enquiry into Arts and the Community, London, Community Development Foundation.

Community Development Journal, an International Journal for Community Workers, Oxford, Oxford University Press.

Duffy, H. (1994), "Empowerment: finding the solution to poverty and social deprivation", in *European Urban Management*, 1, pp.148-151.

Duncan, T. (1990), "Community councils in Glasgow. The development of an urban grassroots democracy", in *Local Government Studies*, March-April, pp. 8-16.

Hain, P. (1980), *Neighbourhood Participation*, London, Temple Smith.

Henderson, P., and Thomas, D. (1980), *Skills in Neighbourhood Work*, London, Allen and Unwin.

Hoggett, P. (1989), "Tenant power in Middlesbrough", in *Chartist*, July-September.

Hoggett, P., and Hambleton, R. (1989), "Local heroes", in *New Statesman and Society*, 5 May.

Hudson, P. (1993), *Managing Your Community Building*, London, Community Matters.

Jacquier, C. (1991), *Voyage dans dix quartiers européens en crise*, Paris, L'Harmattan.

Jankowsky, N. (1982), "Community television: a tool for community action?", in *Communication*, 7, pp. 33-58.

Leonard, P. (ed.) (1975), *The Sociology of Community Action*, Keele, University of Keele.

McConnell, C. (1992), *Promoting Community Development in Europe*, London, Community Development Foundation.

Smith, J. (1992), *Community Development and Tenant Action*, London, National Coalition for Neighbourhoods and the Community Development Foundation.

Taylor, M. (1987), *Community Work in the UK 1982-6*, London, Community Projects Foundation.

Taylor, M. (1992), *Signposts to Community Development*, London, Community Development Foundation and the National Coalition for Neighbourhoods.

Thake, S., and Staubach, R. (1993), *Investing in People. Rescuing Communities from the Margin*, York, Joseph Rowntree Foundation.

Twelvetrees, A. (1976), *Community Associations and Centres. A Comparative Study*, Oxford, Pergamon.

Twelvetrees, A. (1989), *Organizing for Neighbourhood Development. A Comparative Study of Community Development Corporations and Citizen Power Organizations*, Aldershot, Avebury.

Van Rees, *et al.* (1991), *A Survey of Contemporary Community Development in Europe*, The Hague, Hendriks-Stichting.

Wates, N., and Knevitt, C. (1987), *Community Architecture*, Harmondsworth, Penguin.

Willmott, P. (1984), *Community in Social Policy*, London, Policy Studies Institute.

2. Community relations

Council of Europe (1991), *Community and Ethnic Relations in Europe*, final report of the Community Relations project, Strasbourg, Council of Europe.

Cross, M. (1983), "Migrant workers in European cities: concentration, conflict and social policy", paper, Birmingham, SSRC/Research Unit on Ethnic Relations.

Dixon, R. M. (1991), *Black Art, Poverty and the Issue of Equity. A Study of Art and Creative Culture Within Toxteth*, Liverpool, Race & Social Policy Unit, University of Liverpool.

Edwards, J., and Batley, R., *The Politics of Positive Discrimination*, London, Tavistrock.

Glebe, G., and O'Loughlin, J. (eds.) (1987), *Foreign Minorities in Continental European Cities*, Stuttgart, Steiner.

Haest, G. (1989), *De Ouwe Garde, het Andere Slag en de Buitenlanders. De Gesciedenis van een Saneringswijk*, Assen - Maastricht, Van Gorcum.

Jackson, P. (1980), *Ethnic Groups and Boundaries. "Ordered Segmentation" in Urban Neighbourhood*, Oxford, School of Geography, University of Oxford.

Johnson, M., and Cross, M. (1984), "Surveying service users in multi-racial areas", paper, Coventry, Centre for Research in Ethnic Relations.

Khan, N. (1976), *The Arts Britain Ignores. The Arts of Ethnic Minorities in Britain*, London, Community Relations Commission.

Loo, H., van der, Loozen R., and Oosterman J. (1988), *Buurt in Balans. Levensstijlen in nieuw Oudwijk*, Utrecht, Uitgeverij Jan van Arkel.

Poujol, G., and Labourie, R. (eds.) (1979), *Les cultures populaires. Permanences et émergences des cultures minoritaires, locales, ethniques, sociales et religieuses*, Toulouse, Privat.

Pryce, K. (1986), *Endless Pressure. A Study of West Indian Lifestyles in Bristol*, Bristol, Bristol Classic Press.

Rex, J. (1986), *The Concept of A Multi-Cultural Society*, Occasional Papers, Centre for Research in Ethnic Relations, University of Warwick, Coventry.

Rex, J. (1991), "The Political Sociology of a Multi-Cultural Society", in *European Journal for Intercultural Studies*, Vol 1, No 2, Stoke on Trent, Trentham Books.

Rex, J. (1992) *Ethnic Identity and Ethnic Mobilisation in Britain*, Research Monograph No 5, Centre for Research in Ethnic Relations, University of Warwick, Coventry.
Rex, J. (1996 forthcoming), *Ethnic Minorities in the Mordern Nation State*, London, MacMillan.
Rex, J., and Drury, B. (1994), *Ethnic Mobilisation in a Multi-Cultural Europe*, Aldershot, Avebury.
Rex, J., and Moore, R. (1967), *Race, Community and Conflict*, London, Oxford University Press.
Schuringa, L. (1989), *Culturen als Buren*, Utrecht, Uitgeverij Jan van Arkel.
Shaw, A. (1988), *A Pakistani Community in Britain*, Oxford, Blackwell.
Skoog, B. (1983), *Les immigrants et le dévelopement culturel dans les villes européennes*, Strasbourg, Council of Europe.
Toubon, J., and Messamah, K. (1990), *Centralité immigrée. Le quartier de la Goutte d'Or: dynamiques d'un espace pluri-ethnique*, Paris, L'Harmattan.

3. Culture and neighbourhoods

Arts Council of Great Britain (1989), *An Urban Renaissance. Sixteen Case Studies Showing the Role of the Arts in Urban Regeneration*, London, Arts Council.
Bersano, G. (ed.) (1992), *Quale cultura nella periferia metropolitana*, atti del convegno internazionale, Milan, 6-7 April 1990, Milan, Osservatorio Culturale Lombardo/Regione Lombardia.
Bianchini, F., and Parkinson, M. (1993), *Cultural Policy and Urban Regeneration. The West European Experience*, Manchester, Manchester University Press.
Bramham, P., Henry, I., Mommaas, H., and van der Poel, H. (1989), *Leisure and Urban Processes. Critical Studies of Leisure Policy in Western European Cities*, London, Routledge.
Caielli, F. (1985), *La città che vive. Milano dai campi gioco all'animazione di quartiere*, Milano, Centro Culturale Perini.

Clifford, S., and King, A. (1993), *Local Distinctiveness. Place, Particularity and Identity*, London, Common Ground.

Collard, P. (1988), *Arts in Inner Cities*, unpublished report (available from the House of Commons Library), London, The Office of Arts and Libraries.

Community Development Foundation (1992), *Arts and Communities*, report of the National Enquiry into Arts and the Community, London, Community Development Foundation.

Dixon, R. M. (1991), *Black Art, Poverty and the Issue of Equity. A Study of Art and Creative Culture Within Toxteth*, Liverpool, Race & Social Policy Unit, University of Liverpool.

Fuchs, M., and Liebald, C. (1989), *Projektorientierte Künstler-weiterbildung*, Remscheid, Institut für Bildung und Kultur.

Goodey, B. (1983), *Ville et vie culturelle dans les années 80. Rapports et essais provenant du Projet des vingt et unes villes du Conseil de l'Europe*, Strasbourg, Council of Europe.

Greater London Council (1986), *Campaign for a Popular Culture*, London, GLC.

Institut für Bildung und Kultur (1985), *Künstler in der Sozialen Kulturarbeit*, Remscheid, Institut für Bildung und Kultur.

Khan, N. (1976), *The Arts Britain Ignores. The Arts of Ethnic Minorities in Britain*, London, Community Relations Commission.

Kelly, O. (1984), *Community, Art and the State*, London, Comedia.

Lalive d'Epinay, C., Bassand, M., Christe, E., and Gros, D. (1982), "Persistance de la culture populaire dans les sociétés industrielles avancées", in *Revue française de sociologie*, 23, pp. 87-109.

Lewis, J., Morley, D., and Southwood, R. (1986), *Art. Who Needs It? The Audience for Community Arts*, London, Comedia.

Rellstab, U. (1988), *Quartierkultur*, Zürich, Verlag Pro Juventute.

Rizzardo, R. (1984), *Ville et culture. Nouvelles réponses aux problèmes culturels*, Strasbourg, Council of Europe.

Rossel, P., Hainard, F., and Bassand, M., *Cultures et réseaux en périphérie*, Lausanne, Réalités sociales.

Roulleau-Berger, L. (1993), *La ville intervalle. Jeunes entre centre et banlieue.*

Shaw, P. (1992), *Changing Places. The Arts in Scotland's Urban Areas*, Edinburgh, Scottish Arts Council/Scottish Office Industry Department.

Skoog, B. (1983), *Les immigrants et le dévelopement culturel dans les villes européennes*, Strasbourg, Council of Europe.

Unesco (1987), *Culture in the Neighbourhood*, final report of the International Experts Meeting, Baden, 26 September 1986, Bern, Swiss National Commission for UNESCO.

Unesco (1988), *Quartier-Kultur: die Stadt lebt*, final report of the International Experts Meeting, Ruschlikon, 6-7 November 1987, Bern, Swiss National Commission for UNESCO/Gottlieb Duttweiler Institut.

Unesco (1990), *Culture in the Neighbourhood: Cultural Animation in Urban Districts*, final report of the International Experts Meeting, Männedorf, 30 November to 2 December 1989, Bern, Swiss National Commission for UNESCO/BOLDERN, Evangelical Meeting and Study Center.

Unesco (1991), *Culture in the Neighbourhood: Cultural Fringe of the Town*, final report of the European Experts Meeting, Vienna, 20-22 March 1991, Vienna, Austrian Commission for UNESCO.

Unesco (1993), *Culture in the Neighbourhood: the Infrastructure for Neighbourhood Culture*, final report of the International Experts Meeting, Helsinki, 23-25 September 1992, Helsinki, Finnish National Commission for UNESCO.

4. Definitions

Abrams, P. (1982), *Historical Sociology*, Shepton Mallet, Open Books.

Allan, G. A. (1979), *Sociology of Friendship and Kinship*, London, Allen and Unwin.

Berry, B. J. L., and Kasarda, J. D. (1977), *Contemporary Urban Ecology*, New York, Macmillan.

Bulmer, M. (1985), "The rejuvenation of community studies? Neighbours, network and policy", in *The Sociological Review*, 33, pp. 430-448.

Bulmer, M. (1986), *Neighbours. The Work of Philip Abrams*, Cambridge, Cambridge University Press.

Burgess, E. W. (ed.) (1926), *The Urban Community*, Chicago, University of Chicago Press.

Carter, H. (1982), *The Study of Urban Geography*, London, Arnold.

Castells, M. (1983), *The City and the Grassroots. A Cross-Cultural Theory of Urban Social Movements*, London, Arnold.

de Certeau, M. (1980), *L'invention du quotidien. Vol. I*, Paris, 10/18.

Choldin, H. (1985), *Cities and Suburbs. An Introduction to Urban Sociology*, New York, Mc Graw Hill.

Clifford, S., and King, A. (1993), *Local Distinctiveness. Place, Particularity and Identity*, London, Common Ground.

Day, G., and Murdoch, J. (1993), "Locality and community: coming to terms with place", in *The Sociology Review*, 41, pp. 82-111.

Elia, G. (1971), *Sociologia urbana*, Milan, Hoepli.

Evans, B. (1994), "Planning, sustainability and the chimera of community", in *Town and Country Planning*, April.

Fraser, J. (1987), "Community, the private and the individual", in *The Sociology Review*, 35, pp. 795-818.

Giard, L., and Mayol, P. (1980), *L'invention du quotidien. Vol. II: habiter, cuisiner*, Paris, 10/18.

Giddens, A. (1993), *Sociology*, Cambridge, Polity.

Goodall, B. (1987), *Dictionary of Human Geography*, Harmondsworth, Penguin.

Hall, P. (1987), *Urban and Regional Planning*, London, Allen and Unwin.

Hall, P. (1988), *Cities of Tomorrow. An Intellectual History of Urban Planning and Design in the Twentieth Century*, Oxford, Blackwell.

Hallmann, H. W. (1984), *Neighbourhoods. Their Place in Urban Life*, Beverly Hills, Sage.

Hannerz, U. (1980), *Exploring the City. Enquiries towards an Urban Anthropology*, New York, Columbia University Press.

Hannerz, U. (1992), *Cultural Complexity. Studies in the Social Organization of Meaning*, New York, Columbia University Press.

Harvey, D. (1985), *Consciousness and the Urban Experience. Studies in the History and Theory of Capitalist Urbanization*, Oxford, Blackwell.

Joye, D., Grosso Ciponte, A., Richard, J., *et al.* (1992), *Le quartier. Une unité politique et sociale?*, Lausanne, Institut de Recherche sur l'Environnement Construit (IREC).

Keller, S. (1968), *The Urban Neighbourhood*, New York, Random House.

Kelly, O. (1984), *Community, Art and the State*, London, Comedia.

Klein, J. (1956), *The Study of Groups*, London, Routledge & Kegan Paul.

Krupat, E. (1985), *People in Cities. The Urban Environment and its Effects*, Cambridge, Cambridge University Press.

Leonard, P. (ed.) (1975), *The Sociology of Community Action*, Keele, University of Keele.

Lundby, K. (1988), "Cultural identity as basis for community television", in *Nordicom Review of Nordic Mass Communication Research*, 2, pp. 24-30.

Martinotti, G. (1968) (ed.), *Città e analisi sociologica*, Padua, Marsilio.

Oakley, A. (1991), "Social class and social support", in *Sociology*, 25, pp. 31-59.

Ogburn, W. F. (1937), *Sociological Characteristics of Cities*, Chicago, Chicago University Press.

Park, R. E. (1952), *Human Communities. The City and Human Ecology*, New York, Free Press.

Perec, G. (1974), *Espèces d'espaces*, Paris, Galilée.

Pickvance, C. G. (ed.) (1976), *Urban Sociology: Critical Essays*, London, Methuen.

Plant, R. (1974), *Community and Ideology*, London, Routledge and Kegan Paul.

Poujol, G., and Labourie, R. (eds.) (1979), *Les cultures populaires. Permanences et émergences des cultures minoritaires, locales, ethniques, sociales et religieuses*, Toulouse, Privat.

Relph, E. (1976), *Place and Placelessness*, London, Pion.

Robinson, F., and Abrams, P. (1977), *What We Know About the Neighbours?*, Durham, Rowntree Research Unit, University of Durham.

Seabrook, J. (1984), *The Idea of Neighbourhood*, London, Pluto Press.

Sennett, R. (1977), *The Fall of Public Man*, New York, Knopf.

Sennett, R. (1990), *The Conscience of the Eye*, London, Faber and Faber.

Simmel, G., *et al.* (1903), *Die Grossstadt, Vorträge und Aufsätze zur Städteanstellung*, Dresden, Zahn und Jaensch.

Smith, M. P. (1980), *The City and Social Theory*, Oxford, Blackwell.

Smith, R. A. (1975), "Measuring the neighbourhood cohesion: a review and some suggestions", in *Human Ecology*, 3(3), pp. 143-60.

Tuan, Y. (1974), *Topophilia. A Study of Environmental Perceptions, Attitudes and Values*, Eaglewood-Cliffs (NJ), Prentice-Hall.

Tuan, Y. (1977), *Space and Place. The Perspective of Experience*, London, Arnold.

Williams, R. (1976), *Keywords*, London, Fontana.

Wilson, T. C. (1993), "Urbanism and kinship bonds: a test of four generalizations", in *Sociology*, 71, pp. 703-12.

Wirth, L. (1928), *The Ghetto*, Chicago, University of Chicago Press.

Wirth, L. (1938), "Urbanism as a Way of Life", in *American Journal of Sociology*, 44.

Wirth, L. (1964), *On Cities and Social Life. Selected Papers*, edited by A. J. Reiss Jr., Chicago and London, University of Chicago Press.

5. Deprivation

Abrams, P. (1978), *Work, Urbanism and Inequality. UK Society Today*, London, Weinfeld & Nicolson.

Bentham, C. G. (1985), "Which areas have the worst urban problems?", in *Urban Studies*, 2.

Bucneau, P., *et al.* (1989), *Coping with Social and Economic Change at Neighbourhood Level. An Annotated Bibliography*, Shankill, European Foundation for the Improvement of Living and Working Conditions.

Campbell, B. (1993), *Goliath. Britain's Dangerous Places*, London, Methuen.

Cap, E. (1994), "The poverty atlas: regenerating Antwerp's disadvantaged areas", in *European Urban Management*, 1, pp. 152-3.

Castle, B. (1994), "Here be dragons", in *Town and Country Planning*, March, pp. 82-4.

Cohen, A. (ed.) (1986), *Symbolising Boundaries*, Manchester, Manchester University Press.

Cowley, J., *et al.* (eds.) (1977), *Community or Class Struggle?*, London, Stage 1.

Dixon, R. M. (1991), *Black Art, Poverty and the Issue of Equity. A Study of Art and Creative Culture Within Toxteth*, Liverpool, Race & Social Policy Unit, University of Liverpool.

Donnison, D., and Middleton, A. (eds.) (1987), *Regenerating the Inner City. Glasgow's Experience*, London, Routledge and Kegan Paul.

Duffy, H. (1994), "Empowerment: finding the solution to poverty and social deprivation", in *European Urban Management*, 1, pp. 148-151.

Engbersen, G. (1990), "Cultural differentiation in a low income neighbourhood", in Deben, L., Heinemeijer, W., and van der Vaart, D., *Residential Differentiation*, Amsterdam, Centrum voor Grootstedelijk Onderzoek, pp. 202-13.

European Foundation for the Improvement of Living and Working Conditions (1988), *Locally- Based Responses to Long-term Unemployment*, Shankill, EFILW.

Foster, J. (1990), *Villains. Crime and Community in the Inner City*, London, Routledge.

Hall, P. (ed.) (1981), *The Inner City in Context*, London, Heinemann.

Harrison, P. (1985), *Inside the Inner City*, Harmondsworth, Penguin.

Henderson, J., and Kahn, V. (1987), *Race, Class and State Housing. Inequality in the Allocation of Public Housing in Britain*, Aldershot, Gower.

Jacquier, C. (1991), *Voyage dans dix quartiers européens en crise*, Paris, L'Harmattan.

Keating, M. (1988), *The City that Refused to Die [Glasgow]*, Aberdeen University Press.

Lutte, G. (1981), *Giovani invisibili. Lavoro, disoccupazione, vita quotidiana nel quartiere romano della Magliana*, Rome, Lavoro.

Macgregor, S., and Pimlott, B. (1991), *Tackling the Inner Cities. The 1980s Reviewed, Prospects for the 1990s*, Oxford, Clarendon Press.

Michie, J., and Grieve Smith, J. (eds.) (1994), *Unemployment in Europe*, London, Academic Press.

Pilkington, E. (1994), "Ghetto blaster", in *The Guardian Weekend*, 4 June.

Provan, B. (1993), *Problem Housing Estates in Britain*, unpublished Ph.D. thesis, London, London School of Economics.

Reynolds, F. (1986), *A Problem Estate. An Account of Omega and its People*, London, Gower.

Szelenyi, I. (1983), *Urban Inequalities under State Socialism*, Oxford, Oxford University Press.

Thake, S., and Staubach, R. (1993), *Investing in People. Rescuing Communities from the Margin*, York, Joseph Rowntree Foundation.

Wallman, S. (1984), *Eight London Households*, London, Tavistock.

Wilson, J. (1987), *The Truly Disadvantaged. The Inner City, the Underclass and Public Policy*, Chicago, University of Chicago Press.

6. Descriptions of neighbourhood life

Anderson, E. (1990), *Streetwise: Race, Class and Change in an Urban Community*, Chicago, Chicago University Press.

Baroni, A., Boselli, A. M., and Caravello, G. (1979), *Quartiere 4-S. Metodi di ecologia umana applicati all'analisi di un quartiere padovano*, Padua, Patron.

Bishop, J., and Hoggett, P. (1986), *Organizing around Enthusiasms*, London, Comedia.

Burgel, G. (1986), "L'espace résidentiel athénien: les orphelins de l'Etat", in *Espaces- Populations-Sociétés*, vol. 1.

Campbell, B. (1993), *Goliath. Britain's Dangerous Places*, London, Methuen.

Castells, M. (1983), *The City and the Grassroots. A Cross-Cultural Theory of Urban Social Movements*, London, Arnold.

Castle, B. (1994), "Here be dragons", in *Town and Country Planning*, March, pp. 82-4.

de Certeau, M. (1980), *L'invention du quotidien. Vol. I*, Paris, 10/18.

Giard, L., and Mayol, P. (1980), *L'invention du quotidien. Vol. II: habiter, cuisiner*, Paris, 10/18.

Gibson, T. (1984), *Counterweight. The Neighbourhood Opinion*, London, Town and Country Planning Association.

Haest, G. (1989), *De Ouwe Garde, het Andere Slag en de Buitenlanders. De Gesciedenis van een Saneringswijk*, Assen - Maastricht, Van Gorcum.

Hall, P. (ed.) (1981), *The Inner City in Context*, London, Heinemann.

Harrison, P. (1985), *Inside the Inner City*, Harmondsworth, Penguin.

Hurstel, J. (1984), *Jeunes au bistrot, cultures sur macadam*, ed. Syros, collection PEM.

Hurstel, J. (1988), *Chroniques culturelles barbares*, ed. Syros, collection Alternatives.

Incatasciato, B. (1975), *Dalla scuola al quartiere. Il movimento di "Scuola e quartiere" a Firenze (1968-1973)*, Rome, Editori Riuniti.

Jansen, G. H. (1978), *De Straat: Een Portret*, Muiden, Coutinho.

Lalive d'Epinay, C., Bassand, M., Christe, E., and Gros, D. (1982), "Persistance de la culture populaire dans les sociétés industrielles avancées", in *Revue française de sociologie*, 23, pp. 87-109.

Loo, H., van der, Loozen R., and Oosterman J. (1988), *Buurt in Balans. Levensstijlen in nieuw Oudwijk*, Utrecht, Uitgeverij Jan van Arkel.

Lunadei, S. (1992), *Testaccio: un quartiere popolare*, Milan, Angeli.

Lutte, G. (1981), *Giovani invisibili. Lavoro, disoccupazione, vita quotidiana nel quartiere romano della Magliana*, Rome, Lavoro.

Pazzaglini, M. (1989), *San Lorenzo 1881-1981. Storia urbana di un quartiere popolare di Roma*, Rome, Officina.

Pifferi, E., and Marino, A. (1977), *La cortesella. Vita e morte di un quartiere di Como*, Como, Pifferi.

Pryce, K. (1986), *Endless Pressure. A Study of West Indian Lifestyles in Bristol*, Bristol, Bristol Classic Press.

Schuringa, L. (1989), *Culturen als Buren*, Utrecht, Uitgeverij Jan van Arkel.

Sennett, R., (1990), *The Conscience of the Eye*, London, Faber and Faber.

Smith, R. A. (1975), "Measuring the neighbourhood cohesion: a review and some suggestions", in *Human Ecology*, 3(3), pp. 143-60.

Toubon, J., and Messamah, K. (1990), *Centralité immigrée. Le quartier de la Goutte d'Or: dynamiques d'un espace pluri-ethnique*, Paris, L'Harmattan.

Wallman, S. (1984), *Eight London Households*, London, Tavistock.

7. Education

Alexander, K. (1975), *Adult Education. The Challenge of Change*, London, HMSO.

Allen, G., and Martin, I. (1992), *Education and Community. The Politics of Practice*, London, Cassell.

Incatasciato, B. (1975), *Dalla scuola al quartiere. Il movimento di "Scuola e quartiere" a Firenze (1968-1973)*, Rome, Editori Riuniti.

Lovett, T., Clarke, C., and Kilmurray, A. (1983), *Adult Education and Community Action*, London, Croom Helm.

8. Employment and labour market issues

Abrams, P. (1978), *Work, Urbanism and Inequality. UK Society Today*, London, Weinfeld & Nicolson.

Cooke, P. (1983), "Labour market discontinuity and spatial development", in *Progress in Human Geography*, 4.

Engbersen, G. (1990), "Cultural differentiation in a low income neighbourhood", in Deben, L., Heinemeijer, W., and van der Vaart, D., *Residential Differentiation*, Amsterdam, Centrum voor Grootstedelijk Onderzoek, pp. 202-13.

European Foundation for the Improvement of Living and Working Conditions (1988), *Locally Based Responses to Long-term Unemployment*, Shankill, EFILW.

Lutte, G. (1981), *Giovani invisibili. Lavoro, disoccupazione, vita quotidiana nel quartiere romano della Magliana*, Rome, Lavoro.

Michie, J., and Grieve Smith, J. (eds.) (1994), *Unemployment in Europe*, London, Academic Press.

9. Housing

Ball, M., Harloe, M., and Martens, M. (1988), *Housing and Social Change in Europe and the USA*, London, Routledge.

Brownhill, S. (1990), *Developing London Docklands. Another Great Planning Disaster?*, London, Chapman.

Cameron, S. (1992), "Housing, gentrification and urban regeneration", in *Urban Studies*, 29, pp. 3-14.

Cohen, A. (ed.) (1986), *Symbolising Boundaries*, Manchester, Manchester University Press.

Coleman, A.(1985), *Utopia on Trial. Vision and Reality in Planned Housing*, London, Shipman.

Damer, S. (1989), *From Morepark to "Wine Alley". The Rise and Fall of a Glasgow Housing Scheme*, Edinburgh, Edinburgh University Press.

European Foundation for the Improvement of Living and Working Conditions (1991), abstracts of the conference "The Improvement of the Built Environment and Social Integration in Cities", Berlin, 9-11 October 1991, Shankill, EFILW.

Henderson, J., and Kahn, V. (1987), *Race, Class and State Housing. Inequality in the Allocation of Public Housing in Britain*, Aldershot, Gower.

Hoggett, P. (1989), "Tenant power in Middlesbrough", in *Chartist*, July-September.

Hudson, P. (1993), *Managing Your Community Building*, London, Community Matters.

Macgregor, S., and Pimlott, B. (1991), *Tackling the Inner Cities. The 1980s Reviewed, Prospects for the 1990s*, Oxford, Clarendon Press.

Pilkington, E. (1994), "Ghetto blaster", in *The Guardian Weekend*, 4 June.

Provan, B. (1993), *Problem Housing Estates in Britain*, unpublished Ph.D. thesis, London, London School of Economics.

Smidt-Bartel, J., and Meuter, H. (1986), *Der Wohnungsbestand in Grossiedlungen in der Bundesrepublik Deutschland. Quantitative Eckdaten zur Einschätzung der Bedeutung von Grossiedlungen für die Wohnungsversorgung der Bevölkerung und für zukünftige Aufgaben der Stadterneuerung*, Bonn, Bundesforschungsanstalt für Landeskunde und Raumordnung.

Wallman, S. (1984), *Eight London Households*, London, Tavistock.

Wates, N., and Knevitt, C. (1987), *Community Architecture*, Harmondsworth, Penguin.

10. Neighbourhood media

Baehr, H., and Ryan, M. (1984), *Shut Up and Listen! Women and Local Radio*, London, Comedia.

Béaud, P. (1980), *Médias communautaires. Radios et télévisions locales et expériences d'animation audiovisuelle en Europe*, Strasbourg, Council of Europe.

Berrigan, F. (ed.) (1977), *Access. Some Western Models of Community Media*, Liège, Thone.

Bolis, L. (1984), *Local Radio and Television Stations in Europe*, Strasbourg, Council of Europe.

Bredin, M. (1986), *Organizing Alternative Communication. The Context of Community Radio in Britain*, Leicester, Centre for Mass Communication Research, Leicester University.

Browne, D. R. (1988), *What's Local about Local Radio? A Cross-National Comparative Study*, London, International Institute of Communication.

Collard, S. (1990), "Les télévisions communautaires et locales en communauté française de Belgique", in *Guide des Médias*, 4.

Community Radio Association (1990), *Airflash 37*, London, Community Radio Association.

Hollander, E. (1982), *Kleinschalige massacommunicatie: lokale omroepvormen in West Europa*, The Hague, State Pub. Co.

Hollander, E., and Jankowsky, N. (1984), "Community television: charting its course in Europe", paper, Boston, National Federation of Local Cable Programmers.

Jallov, B. (1983), *Women on the Air. Women in Community Radio in Europe*, Roskilde (DK), Roskilde University.

Jankowsky, N. (1982), "Community television: a tool for community action?", in *Communication*, 7, pp. 33-58.

Jankowsky, N. (1982), *Locale Omroep Bijlmermeer. Eindverslag van een veldonderzoek*, Amsterdam, SISWO.

Jankowsky, N. (1982), *Community Television in Amsterdam. Access to, Participation in and Use of the "Locale Omroep Bijlmermeer"*, Amsterdam, University of Amsterdam.

Jankowsky, N., Prehn, O., and Stappers, J. (eds.) (1992), *The People's Voice. Local Radio and Television in Europe*, London, Libbey.

154

Kleinsteuber, H. J., and Sonnenberg, U. (1990), "Beyond public service and private profit. International experience with non-commercial local radio", in *European Journal of Communication*, 5, pp. 87-106.

Lewis, P. M. (1976), *Community Control of Local Radio*, Strasbourg, Council of Europe.

Lewis, P. M., and Booth, J. (1989), *The Invisible Medium. Public, Commercial and Community Radio*, London, Macmillan.

Loensmann, L. (1990), "Community radio and cultural identity. The development of independent radio in Europe", paper, Dublin, International Communication Association.

Lundby, K. (1988), "Cultural identity as basis for community television", in *Nordicom Review of Nordic Mass Communication Research*, 2, pp. 24-30.

Petersen, V., Prehn, O., and Svendsen, E. N. (1988), "Community radio and television in Denmark", paper, Barcelona, International Association of Mass Communication Research.

Prado, E. (1984), "Radio municipales, una experiencia de comunicatión popular", in *Alfoz*, 11, pp. 43-8.

Prado, E. (1985), "Television comunitaria en Catalunya", in *Telos*, 2, pp. 53-8.

Prehn, O. (1990), "Community radio or just local air waves. The development of community radio in Denmark", paper, Dublin, International Communication Association.

Simon, J. P. (1990), "La communication locale. Les médias et les messages", in *Territoires*, 313, pp. 20-54.

Simon, J. P. (1990), "La communication locale. Les hommes et les réseaux", in *Territoires*, 314, pp. 12-51.

Swedborg, B., and Svard, S. (1978), *Neighbourhood Radio and Community Video in Sweden*, Strasbourg, Council of Europe.

Thomas, M. (1981), *Neighbourhood Radio. A new Medium in Sweden*, Uppsala, Department of Sociology, University of Uppsala.

Vidéotrame (1990), "Community, local and regional television stations in the EEC", proceedings of "Colloque International", Namur, Vidéotrame.

Widlok, P. (1988), "A voice for the voiceless. Community radio: Everyman at the microphone", in *Transatlantic Perspective*, 18, pp. 10-2.

11. Neighbourhood politics

Castells, M. (1983), *The City and the Grassroots. A Cross-Cultural Theory of Urban Social Movements*, London, Arnold.

Cowley, J., *et al.* (eds.) (1977), *Community or Class Struggle?*, London, Stage 1.

Cox, K. R. (1988), "Urban social movements and neighbourhood conflicts: mobilization and saturation", in *Urban Geography*, 8, pp. 416-28.

Cox, K. R. and Johnston, R.J. (1982), *Conflict, Politics and the Urban Scene*, London, Longman.

Cross, M. (1983), "Migrant workers in European cities: concentration, conflict and social policy", paper, Birmingham, SSRC/Research Unit on Ethnic Relations.

Duncan, T. (1990), "Community councils in Glasgow. The development of an urban grassroots democracy", in *Local Government Studies*, March-April, pp. 8-16.

Edwards, J., and Batley, R., *The Politics of Positive Discrimination*, London, Tavistock.

Elliott, B., and McCrone, D (1982), *The City: Patterns of Domination and Conflict*, London, Macmillan.

Gibson, T. (1984), *Counterweight. The Neighbourhood Opinion*, London, Town and Country Planning Association.

Hain, P. (1980), *Neighbourhood Participation*, London, Temple Smith.

Harrison, P. (1985), *Inside the Inner City*, Harmondsworth, Penguin.

Hoggett, P., and Hambleton, R. (1989), "Local heroes", in *New Statesman and Society*, 5 May.

Incatasciato, B. (1975), *Dalla scuola al quartiere. Il movimento di "Scuola e quartiere" a Firenze (1968-1973)*, Rome, Editori Riuniti.

Judd, D., and Parkinson, M. (eds.) (1990), *Leadership and Urban Regeneration. Cities in North America and Europe*, London, Sage.
Loney, M. (1983), *Community Against Government*, London, Heinemann.
Longo, G., Morales, G., and Stefanini, M. (1980), *I consigli di quartiere. Il decentramento e la partecipazione*, Rome, Edizioni delle Autonomie.
Twelvetrees, A. (1985), *Democracy and the Neighbourhood*, London, National Federation of Community Organizations.
Twelvetrees, A. (1989), *Organizing for Neighbourhood Development. A Comparative Study of Community Development Corporations and Citizen Power Organizations*, Aldershot, Avebury.

12. Neighbourhood regeneration

Anderiesen, G., and Reijndorp, A. (1990), "The stabilization of heterogeneity: urban renewal areas in Amsterdam and Rotterdam", in Deben, L., Heinemeijer, W., and van der Vaart, D., *Residential Differentiation*, Amsterdam, Centrum voor Grootstedelijk Onderzoek, pp. 224-34.
Bianchini, F., and Parkinson, M. (1993), *Cultural Policy and Urban Regeneration. The West European Experience*, Manchester, Manchester University Press.
Bishop, B. (1991), *The City in Western Europe. Towards the Ideal European City*, Leeds, Leeds City Council.
Bucneau, P., *et al.* (1989), *Coping with Social and Economic Change at Neighbourhood Level. An Annotated Bibliography*, Shankill, European Foundation for the Improvement of Living and Working Conditions.
Cameron, S. (1992), "Housing, gentrification and urban regeneration", in *Urban Studies*, 29, pp. 3-14.
Cap, E. (1994), "The poverty atlas: regenerating Antwerp's disadvantaged areas", in *European Urban Management*, 1, pp. 152-3.

Castro, R. (1994), *Civilisation urbaine ou barbarie*, Paris, Plon.

Donnison, D., and Middleton, A. (eds.) (1987), *Regenerating the Inner City. Glasgow's Experience*, London, Routledge and Kegan Paul.

European Foundation for the Improvement of Living and Working Conditions (1991), abstracts of the conference "The Improvement of the Built Environment and Social Integration in Cities", Berlin, 9-11 October 1991, Shankill, EFILW.

Falk, N. (1992), *Voluntary Work and the Environment: Local Environmental Development Initiatives in Europe*, Shankill, European Foundation for the Improvement of Living and Working Conditions.

Henderson, J., and Kahn, V. (1987), *Race, Class and State Housing. Inequality in the Allocation of Public Housing in Britain*, Aldershot, Gower.

Judd, D., and Parkinson, M. (eds.) (1990), *Leadership and Urban Regeneration. Cities in North America and Europe*, London, Sage.

Keating, M. (1988), *The City that Refused to Die [Glasgow]*, Aberdeen, Aberdeen University Press.

Levy, F. (1989), *Bilan-perspective des contrats de plan de développement social des quartiers*, Paris, La Documentation Française.

Lawless, P. (1989), *Britain's Inner Cities*, London, Chapman.

Lewis, N. (1990), *Inner City Regeneration*, London, Open University Press.

Macgregor, S., and Pimlott, B. (1991), *Tackling the Inner Cities. The 1980s Reviewed, Prospects for the 1990s*, Oxford, Clarendon Press.

Menanteau, J. (1994), *Les banlieues*, Ivry-sur-Seine, Le Monde.

Thake, S., and Staubach, R. (1993), *Investing in People. Rescuing Communities from the Margin*, York, Joseph Rowntree Foundation.

13.   Social networks

Allan, G. A. (1979), *Sociology of Friendship and Kinship*, London, Allen and Unwin.

Baroni, A., Boselli, A. M., and Caravello, G. (1979), *Quartiere 4-S. Metodi di ecologia umana applicati all'analisi di un quartiere padovano*, Padua, Patron.

Bishop, J., and Hoggett, P. (1986), *Organizing around Enthusiasms*, London, Comedia.

Bulmer, M. (1985), "The rejuvenation of community studies? Neighbours, network and policy", in *The Sociological Review*, 33, pp. 430-448.

Bulmer, M. (1986), *Neighbours. The Work of Philip Abrams*, Cambridge University Press.

Campbell, K. E., and Lee, B. A. (1992), "Sources of personal neighbourhood networks: social integration, need or time", in *Social Forces*, 70, pp. 1360-80.

Fischer, C., *et al.* (1977), *Network and Places. Social Relations in the Urban Setting*, New York, Free Press.

Oakley, A. (1991), "Social class and social support", in *Sociology*, 25, pp. 31-59.

Robinson, F., and Abrams, P. (1977), *What We Know About the Neighbours?*, Durham, Rowntree Research Unit, University of Durham.

Scott, J. (1991), *Social Network Analysis. A Handbook*, London, Sage.

Smith, R. A. (1975), "Measuring the neighbourhood cohesion: a review and some suggestions", in *Human Ecology*, 3(3), pp. 143-60.

Van Rees, *et al.* (1991), *A Survey of Contemporary Community Development in Europe*, The Hague, Hendriks-Stichting.

Wellman, B., and Berkowitz, S.D. (eds.) (1988), *Social Structure: a Network Approach*, Cambridge, Cambridge University Press.

Willmott, P. (1987), *Friendship, Networks and Social Support*, London, Policy Studies Institute.

Wilson, T. C. (1993), "Urbanism and kinship bonds: a test of four generalizations", in *Sociology*, 71, pp. 703-12.

14. Social policy

Chevallier, M. (1986), *Test des instruments d'évaluation proposés par le groupe "Evaluation des politiques sociales au niveau local" du Commissariat Général au Plan*, Lyons, Arcades.

La Documentation Française (1986), *Les politiques sociales transversales, une méthodologie d'évaluation de leurs effets locaux*, Paris, La Documentation Française.

Thake, S., and Staubach, R. (1993), *Investing in People. Rescuing Communities from the Margin*, York, Joseph Rowntree Foundation.

Willmott, P. (1984), *Community in Social Policy*, London, Policy Studies Institute.

15. Social stratification

Amendola, G. (1985), *Segni e evidenze. Atlante sociale di Bari*, Bari, Dedalo.

Campbell, B. (1993), *Goliath. Britain's Dangerous Places*, London, Methuen.

Cap, E. (1994), "The poverty atlas: regenerating Antwerp's disadvantaged areas", in *European Urban Management*, 1, pp. 152-3.

Dahrendorf, R. (1989), "The future of the underclass: a European perspective", in *Northern Economic Review*, 18.

Jackson, P. (1980), *Ethnic Groups and Boundaries. "Ordered Segmentation" in Urban Neighbourhood*, Oxford, School of Geography, University of Oxford.

Johnson, M, and Cross, M. (1984), "Surveying service users in multiracial areas", paper, Coventry, Centre for Research in Ethnic Relations.

Saunders, P. (1990), *Social Class and Stratification*, London, Routledge.

Wellman, B., and Berkowitz S. D. (eds.) (1988), *Social Structure: a Network Approach*, Cambridge, Cambridge University Press.

16. Sustainability issues

Christie, I., and Ritchie, N. (1992), *Energy Efficiency. The Policy Agenda for the 1990s*, London, Policy Studies Institute/ Neighbourhood Energy Action.

Energy Action, bulletin of the Neighbourhood Energy Action, Newcastle-upon-Tyne, Neighbourhood Energy Action.

Falk, N. (1992), *Voluntary Work and the Environment: Local Environmental Development Initiatives in Europe*, Shankill, European Foundation for the Improvement of Living and Working Conditions.

17. Voluntary sector

Baine, S., Benington, J., and Russell, J. (1992), *Changing Europe. Challenges Facing the Voluntary and Community Sectors in the 1990s*, London, NCVO.

Besset, T. (1991), *Associations de quartier traditionnelles à Berne et à Genève. Contribution à une étude de la sociabilité urbaine*, Lausanne, Institut de Recherche sur l'Environnement Construit.

Bishop, J., and Hoggett, P. (1986), *Organizing around Enthusiasms,* London, Comedia.

Bulmer, M. (1986), *Neighbours. The Work of Philip Abrams*, Cambridge, Cambridge University Press.

Campbell, B. (1993), *Goliath. Britain's Dangerous Places*, London, Methuen.

Chanan, G. (1992), *Out of the Shadows. Local Community Action and the European Community*, final report of the research project "Coping with Social and Economic Change at Neighbourhood Level", Luxembourg, Office for Official Publications of the European Communities.

Christie, I., and Ritchie, N. (1992), *Energy Efficiency. The Policy Agenda for the 1990s*, London, Policy Studies Institute/Neighbourhood Energy Action.

Falk, N. (1992), *Voluntary Work and the Environment: Local Environmental Development Initiatives in Europe*, Shankill, European Foundation for the Improvement of Living and Working Conditions.

Harvey, B. (1992), *Networking in Europe. A Guide to European Voluntary Organizations*, London, NCVO/Community Development Foundation.

Henderson, P., and Thomas, D. (1980), *Skills in Neighbourhood Work*, London, Allen and Unwin.

Hoggett, P. (1989), "Tenant power in Middlesbrough", in *Chartist*, July-September.

Hoggett, P., and Hambleton, R. (1989), "Local heroes", in *New Statesman and Society*, 5 May.

Humphrey, R., and Snaith, R. (1982), "Activate thy neighbour", in *Voluntary Action*, Spring, pp. 33-34.

Institut für Bildung und Kultur (1985), *Künstler in der Sozialen Kulturarbeit*, Remscheid, Institut für Bildung und Kultur.

Jacquier, C. (1991), *Voyage dans dix quartiers européens en crise*, Paris, L'Harmattan.

Acknowledgments

We wish to thank the Polytechnic of Bari for the financial support provided for Massimo Torrigiani; and Caterina Fortunato from the Libreria Editrice Universitaria in Bari and Nick Jewson from the Department of Sociology at the University of Leicester for bibliographical advice.

Appendix I

List of Cities and Neighbourhoods
taking part in the "Culture and Neighbourhoods" Project

City	Neighbourhoods
Athens	▸ Patissia ▸ Athens Historic District
Bilbao	▸ Bilbao La Vieja ▸ Deusto
Budapest	▸ Inner City Slum: parts of VIth district, VIIth district and VIIIth district ▸ Havanna Housing Estate (XVIII district) ▸ Pesthidegkut (IInd district)
Copenhagen	▸ Vesterbro ▸ North-West District
Liverpool	▸ Speke ▸ Vauxhall
Lisbon	▸ Alfama ▸ Campo Grande
Marseilles	▸ Panier ▸ Saint-Barthelemy

Munich	▶ Sendling
	▶ Hasenbergl
	▶ Fürstenried
Prague	▶ Prague 7
	▶ Jihozapadni Mesto
Sofia	▶ Oborichte
	▶ Ovtcha Koupel
Turin	▶ San Salvario
	▶ Nizza - Millefonti
Vienna	▶ Augartenviertel
	▶ Alsergrund

Appendix II

List of City Co-ordinators
and Advisers to the Project

City Co-ordinators

Athens
Mr Evangelos GAVRIELATOS
Town Planning Department, Municipality of Athens,
Palaologou 9, GR - 10438 Athens (Greece)

Bilbao
Mrs Ana GOYTIA PRAT
Mr Roberto SAN SALVADOR DEL VALLE
Universidad de Deusto, Instituto Interdisciplinar de Estudios de Ocio,
Apartado 1, E - 48080 Bilbao (Spain)

Budapest
Mr János LADÂNYI
Associated Professor,
University of Economics of Budapest, Department of Sociology,
Fövam ter 8, H - 1093 Budapest (Hungary)

Copenhagen
Mr Thomas Visby SNITKER
Department of Culture, Copenhagen City Hall,
DK - 1599 Copenhagen V (Denmark)

Lisbon
Mr José Paulo CAMPINO
Département du Patrimoine Culturel,
Camara Municipal, Palacio Corucheus,
Rua Alberto de Oliveira, P - 1700 Lisboa (Portugal)

Liverpool
Mr Roger HILL
The Arts of Life, 12A Gambier Terrace,
GB - Liverpool L1 7BL (United Kingdom)

Marseilles
Mr Gilbert CECCALDI
Chargé de mission politique de la ville,
Direction générale des Affaires culturelles de la ville de Marseille,
38 rue Saint-Ferréol, F - 13001 Marseille (France)

Munich
Mr Heiner ZAMETZER
Kulturreferat der Stadt München,
Rindermarkt 3-4, D - 80331 München (Germany)

Prague
Mr Tomáš Adam KUPEC
Studio Barentdorff, Movie Technology,
Veveskova 25, 17000 Praha 7 (Czech Republic)

Sofia
Mr Georgy ROUSKOV
Regional Mayor, Municipality "Ovcha Koupel"-Sofia,
Tzar Boris III Str. 136-B, BG - 1218 Sofia   (Bulgaria)

Turin
Mr Paolo CAMERA
Fonctionnaire du Secteur Administratif,
Chargé de la Décentralisation, Comune di Torino - Settore 20°,
Piazza Palazzo di Città 1, I - 10122 Torino (Italy)

Vienna
Mr Bernhard DENSCHER
Head, Department for Cultural Affairs of the City of Vienna,
- MA7, Rathaus, A - 1082 Wien (Austria)

City Co-ordinators also acting as Project Advisers

Mr János LADÁNYI
Associated Professor,
University of Economics, Department of Sociology,
Fövam ter 8, H - 1093 Budapest (Hungary)

Mr Roberto SAN SALVADOR DEL VALLE
Universidad de Deusto, Instituto Interdisciplinar de Estudios de Ocio,
Apartado 1, E - 48080 Bilbao (Spain)

Mr Heiner ZAMETZER
Kulturreferat der Stadt München,
Rindermarkt 3-4, D - 80331 München (Germany)

Project Advisers

Prof. Giandomenico AMENDOLA
Facoltà di Architettura, Politecnico di Bari,
Strada Verrone 20, I - 70122 Bari (Italy)

Mr Ugo BACCHELLA
Presidente, Fitzcarraldo,
Corso Mediterraneo 94, I - 10129 Torino (Italy)

Prof. MICHEL BASSAND
Directeur de l'Institut de Recherche sur l'Environnement Construit (IREC),
Ecole polytechnique fédérale de Lausanne (EPFL),
Case postale 555, CH - 1001 Lausanne (Switzerland)

Mr Franco BIANCHINI
School of Arts & Humanities, De Montfort University,
Gateway House, The Gateway, GB - Leicester LE1 9BH (United Kingdom)

Mr Geoffrey BROWN
Director, EUCLID,
19 Hope Street, GB - Liverpool L1 9BQ (United Kingdom)

Mr Eduard DELGADO i CLAVERA,
Project Director for Culture and Neighbourhoods
Director, Interarts, Ronda Universitat,
17 pral. 3ª, E - 08007 Barcelona (Spain)

Mr Brian GOODEY
School of Planning, Oxford Brookes University,
Gipsy Lane Campus, GB - Headington Oxford OX3 OBP (United Kingdom)

Mr Benoît GUILLEMONT
Conseiller - Action Culturelle,
Direction Régionale des Affaires Culturelles Rhône-Alpes (DRAC),
6 quai Saint-Vincent, F - 69283 Lyon Cedex 01 (France)

Mr Jean HURSTEL
Directeur, La Laiterie,
Centre européen de la Jeune Création,
15 rue du Hohwald, F - 67000 Strasbourg (France)

Mrs Yvette LECOMTE
Inspectrice, Service de l'Inspection, Ministère de la Culture
et des Affaires sociales de la Communauté française de Belgique,
Rue Louvrex 46 B, B - 4000 Liège (Belgium)

Mr Xavier MARCE
Aribau 324, 6è, 2a, E - 08006 Barcelona (Spain)

Mrs Ursula RELLSTAB
Commission nationale suisse pour l'Unesco,
Rigistrasse 26, CH - 8006 Zürich (Switzerland)

Appendix III

List of Documents established within the Project

- ▸ Project Definition for 1993-1994 Programme
  - Secretariat Memorandum   *Decs-Cult (92) 10*

- ▸ First meeting of the Group of Advisers
  - Minutes   *Decs-Cult/CP (93) 1*

- ▸ Restricted Meeting of the Group of Advisers
  - Summary of Conclusions   *Decs-Cult/CP (93) 4*

- ▸ Towards a Methodology for the Project
  (Working Paper)   *Decs-Cult/CP (93) 5*

- ▸ Towards a Methodology for the Project
  (Working Paper-revised version)   *Decs-Cult/CP (93) 5 rev.*

- ▸ Towards a Methodology for the Project
  (Working Paper-revised version 2)   *Decs-Cult/CP (93) 5 rev.2*

- ▸ Meeting to Launch the Project
  - Summary of Conclusions   *Decs-Cult/CP (93) 6*

- ▸ Towards a Methodology for the Project
  - Author's guide to the working document   *Decs-Cult/CP (93) 9*

- ▸ First Project Conference on "The Urban Space
  and Cultural Policy" (Munich, 17-19 January 1994)
  - Contributions from the Experts
    (Background Document)   *Decs-Cult/CP (94) 1 Def.*

Appendix IV

List of Participants at the First and Second Project Conferences

List of Participants
at the First Project Conference
on "The Urban Space and Cultural Policies"
Munich (Germany), 17 - 19 January 1994

Group of Advisers

Mr Giandomenico AMENDOLA, Facoltà di Architettura, Politecnico di Bari, Strada Verrone 20, I-70122 Bari, Tel: 39-80 523 6171, Fax: 39-80 521 5051

Mr Michel BASSAND, Directeur de L'IREC, Ecole polytechnique fédérale de Lausanne (EPFL), Case postale 555, 14 av. de l'Eglise anglaise, CH-1001 Lausanne, Tel: 41-21 693 32 43, Fax: 41-21 693 38 40

Mr Franco BIANCHINI, School of Arts & Humanities, De Montfort University, Gateway House, The Gateway, GB-Leicester LE1 9BH, Tel: 44-533 577 391, Fax: 44-533 577 199

Mr Brian GOODEY, School of Planning, Oxford Brookes University, Gipsy Lane Campus, GB-Headington Oxford OX3 OBP, Tel: 44-865 483 403, Fax: 44-865 483 298

Mr Benoît GUILLEMONT, Conseiller Action Culturelle, Direction régionale des Affaires culturelles Rhône-Alpes, 6 quai Saint-Vincent, F-69001 Lyons, Tel: 33-72 00 44 17, Fax: 33-72 00 43 30

Mr Jean HURSTEL, Directeur, La Laiterie, Centre européen de la Jeune Création, 15 rue du Hohwald, F-67000 Strasbourg, Tel: 33-88 75 10 05, Fax : 33-88 75 58 78

Mrs Yvette LECOMTE, Inspectrice, Service de l'Inspection, Ministère de la Culture et des Affaires sociales de la Communauté française, 463 rue Louvrex, B-4000 Liege, Tel: 32-41 224 312, Fax: 32-41 231 987

Mr Xavier MARCÉ, Francesc de Moragues 3-5 Pp 1$_a$, L'Hospitalet de Llobregat, E-08901 Barcelona, Tel: 34-3 415 20 72, Fax: 34-3 218 17 30

Mrs Ursula RELLSTAB, Commission nationale suisse pour l'Unesco, Rigistrasse 26, CH-8006 Zürich, Tel: 41-1 361 61 48, Fax: 41-1 361 61 29

Project Co-ordinators

Athens: **Mr Evangelos GAVRIELATOS**   (Apologised for absence)
Town Planning Department, Municipality of Athens, Palaologou 9, GR-10438 Athens, Fax: 30-1 524 71 72

Bilbao: **Ms Ana GOYTIA PRAT**
Universidad de Deusto, Instituto Interdisciplinar de Estudios de Ocio, Apartado 1, E - 48080 Bilbao, Tel: 34-4 445 31 00, Fax: 34-4 445 89 16

Budapest: **Mr János LADÁNYI**
Associated Professor, University of Economics, Department of Sociology, Fövám tér 8, H - 1093 Budapest, Tel/Fax: 36-1 217 51 72

Copenhagen: **Mr Thomas Visby SNITKER**
Department of Culture, Copenhagen City Hall, DK - 1599 Copenhagen V, Tel: 45-33 66 20 80, Fax: 45-33 32 80 64

Lisbon: **Mr José Paulo CAMPINO**
Département du Patrimoine Culturel, Camara Municipal de Lisboa, Praça do Municipio, P-1194 Lisbon, Tel: 351-1 795 16 99, Fax: 351-1 795 17 99

Liverpool: **Mr Nicholas STANLEY**
Councillor, Liverpool City Council, 12 Falkner Street, GB-Liverpool L8, Tel: 44-51 70 87 441, Fax: 44-51 70 93 515

Marseilles: **Mr Hervé MARIOTTI**   (Apologised for absence)
Directeur des Affaires culturelles de la Ville de Marseille, 38 rue St Ferréol,
F-13001 Marseilles, Tel: 33-91 33 03 00, Fax: 33-91 33 14 22

Munich: **Mr Heiner ZAMETZER**
Kulturreferat der Stadt München, Rindermarkt 3-4, D - 8000 Munich 2,
Tel: 49-89 233 62 40, Fax: 49-89 233 86 45

Prague: **Mr Tomáš Adam KUPEC**
Deputy Mayor of Prague 7, District Council, nábř. kpt. Jaroše 1000,
170 05 Prague 7, Czech Republic, Tel: 42-2 371 029, Fax : 42-2 389 2539

Sofia: **Mr Emil LOSEV**
Chef de Cabinet du Maire et des Relations internationales, Municipalité de la
Grande Sofia, 13 Moskovska Street, BG-1000 Sofia, Tel: 359-2 875 813,
Fax: 359-2 870 968

Turin: **Mr Ugo BACCHELLA**
President, Fitzcarraldo, Corso Mediterraneo 94, I-10129 Turin,
Tel: 39 11 581 7232, Fax: 39 11 503 361

Vienna: **Mr Bernhard DENSCHER**   (Apologised for absence)
Head of the Department for Cultural Affairs of the City of Vienna (MA7),
Rathaus, A-1082 Vienna, Tel: 43-1 4000 84711, Fax: 43-1 4000 7216

Also invited

Mr Adele BIANCO, Politecnico di Bari, C/o Prof. G. Amendola, Private
address: Via Villa Torlonia 6/10, I-00161 Roma, Tel (home): 39-6 440 48 55

Mrs Marie BRITTEN, Chargée de Mission du Ministère de la Culture à la
Délégation interministérielle à l'Insertion des Jeunes, 194 av. du Pt Wilson,
F-93217 La-Plaine-St-Denis, Tel: 33-1 49 17 47 32, Fax: 33-1 49 17 47 48

Mr Geoffrey BROWN, EUCLID, 6 Bluecoat Chambers, School Lane,
GB-Liverpool L1 3BX, Tel: 44-51 709 25 64, Fax: 44-51 709 25 75

Mr Josep FORNÉS, Head of Cultural Services in Barcelona (District 6)

Mr Jon GANGOITI URRUTIA, Vice-Mayor of Bilbao (Culture Department), Town Hall of Bilbao, Plaza de Erkoreka s/n, E-Bilbao Vizcaya, Tel: 34-4 446 00 04, Fax: 34-4 446 73 14

Ms Nikki GAVRON, 17 Broadlands Road, GB-London N6 4AE, Tel: 44-81 340 48 20, Fax: 44-81 341 93 47

Mr Dominique JOYE, Politologue, Institut de Recherche sur l'Environnement construit, Ecole Polytechique Fédérale de Lausanne, Case postale 555, CH-1001 Lausanne, Tel: 41-21 693 34 09, Fax: 41-21 693 38 40

Mr Massimo TORRIGIANI, Visiting Research Fellow, De Montfort University, Gateway House, The Gateway, GB-Leicester LE1 9BH,

Ms Felicja MUSIOL-ZUBER, Sociologist, Culture Researcher, Institute of Culture, Senatorska 13/15, P-00 075 Warsaw, Tel/Fax: 48-22 262 477

Council of Europe

CLRAE (Standing Conference on Local and Regional Authorities of Europe)
M. Moreno BUCCI
Vice-president of the Committee on Culture, Education and the Media, Quartier Allende 7, I-55049 Viareggio, Fax: 39-584 49 644

Cultural Policy and Action Division   Fax: 33-88 41 27 88
(Directorate of Education, Culture and Sport)

Mr Eduard DELGADO, Programme Adviser
Ms Kathrin MERKLE, Administrator   Tel: 33-88 41 28 84

**List of participants
at the Second Project Conference
on "Urban Regeneration in European Neighbourhoods"
Bilbao (Spain), 16 - 19 June 1994**

Group of Advisers

Prof. Giandomenico AMENDOLA, Facoltà di Architettura, Politecnico di
Bari, Strada Verrone 20, I-70122 Bari, Tel: 39 80 523 6171,
Fax: 39 80 521 5051

Prof. Michel BASSAND (Apologised for absence)
Directeur de L'IREC, Ecole polytechnique fédérale de Lausanne (EPFL),
Case postale 555, 14 av. de l'Eglise anglaise, CH-1001 Lausanne,
Tel: 41 21 693 32 43, Fax: 41 21 693 38 40

Mr Franco BIANCHINI, School of Arts & Humanities, De Montfort University,
Gateway House, The Gateway, GB-Leicester LE1 9BH, Tel: 44 533 577 391,
Fax: 44 533 577 199

Mr Eduard DELGADO i CLAVERA
Project Director for "Culture and Neighbourhoods"
Deputació de Barcelona, Rambla de Catalunya 126, E-08023 Barcelona,
Tel: 34 3 402 22 29, Fax: 34 3 402 22 98

Prof. Brian GOODEY, School of Planning, Oxford Brookes University, Gipsy
Lane Campus, GB-Headington Oxford OX3 OBP, Tel: 44 865 483 403,
Fax: 44 865 483 298

Mr Benoît GUILLEMONT, Conseiller Action Culturelle, Direction régionale
des Affaires culturelles Rhône-Alpes, 6 quai St-Vincent, F-69001 Lyons,
Tel: 33 72 00 44 17, Fax: 33 72 00 43 30

Mr Jean HURSTEL, Directeur, La Laiterie, Centre européen de la Jeune
Création, 15 rue du Hohwald, F-67000 Strasbourg, Tel: 33 88 75 10 05,
Fax : 33 88 75 58 78

Mrs Yvette LECOMTE, Inspectrice, Service de l'Inspection, Ministère de la Culture et des Affaires sociales de la Communauté française de Belgique, rue Louvrex 46B, B-4000 Liège, Tel: 32 41 22 43 12, Fax: 32 41 23 19 87

Mr Xavier MARCÉ, Francesc de Moragues 3-5 Pp 1$_a$, L'Hospitalet de Llobregat, E-08901 Barcelona, Tel: 34 3 415 20 72, Fax: 34 3 218 17 30

Mrs Ursula RELLSTAB, Commission nationale suisse pour l'Unesco, Rigistrasse 26, CH-8006 Zürich, Tel: 41 1 361 61 48, Fax: 41 1 361 61 29

Project Co-ordinators

Athens: **Mr Evangelos GAVRIELATOS** (Apologised for absence)
Town Planning Department, Municipality of Athens, Palaologou 9, GR-10438 Athens, Fax: 30 1 524 71 72

Bilbao: **Mrs Ana GOYTIA PRAT**
Universidad de Deusto, Instituto Interdisciplinar de Estudios de Ocio, Apartado 1, E-48080 Bilbao, Tel: 34 4 445 31 00, Fax: 34 4 445 89 16

Budapest: **Prof. János LADÁNYI**
Associated Professor, University of Economics, Department of Sociology, Fövam ter 8, H-1093 Budapest, Tel/Fax: 36 1 217 51 72

Copenhagen: **Mr Thomas Visby SNITKER** (Apologised for absence)
Department of Culture, Copenhagen City Hall, DK-1599 Copenhagen V, Tel: 45 33 66 20 80, Fax: 45 33 32 80 64

Lisbon: **Mr José Paulo CAMPINO** (Apologised for absence)
Département du Patrimoine Culturel, Camara Municipal de Lisboa, Palacio Corucheus, Rua Alberto de Oliveira, P-1700 Lisbon, Tel: 351 1 795 16 99, Fax: 351 1 795 17 99

Liverpool: **Mr Roger HILL**
The Arts of Life, 12A Gambier Terrace, GB-Liverpool, Tel: 44 51 709 4403

Marseilles: **Mr Robert VERHEUGE**
Directeur de l'Office de la Culture de Marseille, 38 rue St Ferréol,
F-13001 Marseilles, Tel: 33 91 33 33 79, Fax: 33 91 54 28 84

Munich: **Mr Heiner ZAMETZER**   (Apologised for absence)
Kulturreferat der Stadt München, Rindermarkt 3-4, D - 80331 Munichj,
Tel: 49 89 233 62 40, Fax: 49 89 233 86 45

Prague: **Mr Tomáš Adam KUPEC**
Deputy Mayor of Prague 7, District Council, nábř. kpt. Jaroše 1000,
170 05 Prague 7, Czech Republic, Tel: 42 2 371 029, Fax : 42 2 389 2539

Sofia: **Mr Georgy ROUSKOV**
Mayor of the Outcha Kupel District, Sofia Great Municipality, Tzar Boris III
blv. 136B, BG-1118 Sofia, Tel: 359 2 556 161, Fax: 359 2 575 036

Turin: **Mr Ugo BACCHELLA**
President, Fitzcarraldo, Corso Mediterraneo 94, I-10129 Turin,
Tel: 39 11 568 33 65, Fax: 39 11 503 361

Vienna: **Dr Bernhard DENSCHER**
Head of the Department for Cultural Affairs of the City of Vienna (MA7),
Rathaus, A-1082 Vienna, Tel: 43 1 4000 84711, Fax: 43 1 4000 7216

Also invited

Mr Gavier ATANCE, BENECE, E-Barcelona, Fax: 34 3 284 00 75

Ms Marie DAVIDSON, Arts Development Officer, Department of Performing
Arts and Venues, Glasgow City Council, Candleriggs, GB-Glasgow G1 1NQ,
Tel: 44 41 227 5429, Fax: 44 41 227 5533

Mr Josep FORNÉS GARCIA, Tecnic Staffculture, Ayuntamiento de Barcelona, Districte de Gracia, Topazi 36 Atic, E-08012 Barcelona, Tel: 34 3 415 26 25

Ms Ria LAVRIJSEN (Apologised for absence)
Soeterijn/Plateforms for Non-Western Cultures, Royal Tropical Institute, NL - Amsterdam, Fax: 31 20 568 8384

Mr Jon LEONARDO, Faculté de Sociologie, Université de Deusto, Avenue Universidades s/n, E-48080 Bilbao, Tel: 34 4 445 31 00,Fax: 34 4 445 89 16

Dr Jan OOSTERMAN, Rotterdam City Council, Dep. of Urban Planning and Housing, Section Urban Planning, Traffic and Transportation, PO Box 6699, NL-3002 AR Rotterdam, Tel: 31 10 489 6432, Fax: 31 10 489 5168

Mr Miquel SANLLEHY GARCIA, Coordinador de fernicios, Distrito de Graciz (Ayuntamento de Barcelona), Pl. rius i Taulet n° 2, E-Barcelona, Tel: 34 3 415 2625

Mrs Liliane SCHAUSS, Chargée des Echanges culturels internationaux, Office de la Culture de Marseille, 38 rue St-Ferreol, F-13001 Marseilles, Tel: 33 91 33 33 79, Fax: 33 91 54 28 84

City of Bilbao

Town Hall
Plaza de Erkoreka s/n, E-Bilbao Vizcaya,
Tel: 34 4 446 00 04, Fax: 34 4 446 73 14

Mr Ibon ARESO, Vice-Mayor for Urban Planning
Mr Jon GANGOITI URRUTIA, Vice-Mayor for Culture
Ms Mercedes MENDIZABAL, Cultural Management, Culture Area
Ms Maria Victoria ZABALETA, Director of the Culture Area

Deusto University
Instituto de Estudios de Ocio, Apart. 1, E-48080 Bilbao,
Tel: 34 4 445 31 00, Fax: 34 4 445 89 16

Ms Ana GOYTIA PRAT
Mr Roberto SAN SALVADOR DEL VALLE
Ms Mercedes RODRIGUEZ

Council of Europe
Palais de l'Europe, F-67075 Strasbourg Cedex,
Tel: 33 88 41 20 00, Fax: 33 88 41 27 82

Culture Committee
Mr Norbert RIEDL, Chairman

Cultural Policy and Action Division   Fax: 33 88 41 27 88
(Directorate of Education, Culture and Sport)

Ms Kathrin MERKLE, Administrator   Tel: 33 88 41 28 84
Mlle Evelyne PORRI, Assistant

Sales agents for publications of the Council of Europe
Agents de vente des publications du Conseil de l'Europe

AUSTRALIA/AUSTRALIE
Hunter publications, 58A, Gipps Street
AUS-3066 COLLINGWOOD, Victoria
Fax: (61) 34 19 71 54

AUSTRIA/AUTRICHE
Gerold und Co., Graben 31
A-1011 WIEN 1
Fax: (43) 1512 47 31 29

BELGIUM/BELGIQUE
La Librairie européenne SA
50, avenue A. Jonnart
B-1200 BRUXELLES 20
Fax: (32) 27 35 08 60

Jean de Lannoy
202, avenue du Roi
B-1060 BRUXELLES
Fax: (32) 25 38 08 41

CANADA
Renouf Publishing Company Limited
1294 Algoma Road
CDN-OTTAWA ONT K1B 3W8
Fax: (1) 613 741 54 39

DENMARK/DANEMARK
Munksgaard
PO Box 2148
DK-1016 KØBENHAVN K
Fax: (45) 33 12 93 87

FINLAND/FINLANDE
Akateeminen Kirjakauppa
Keskuskatu 1, PO Box 218
SF-00381 HELSINKI
Fax: (358) 01 21 44 35

GERMANY/ALLEMAGNE
UNO Verlag
Poppelsdorfer Allee 55
D-53115 BONN
Fax: (49) 228 21 74 92

GREECE/GRÈCE
Librairie Kauffmann
Mavrokordatou 9, GR-ATHINAI 106 78
Fax: (30) 13 83 03 20

HUNGARY/HONGRIE
Euro Info Service
Magyarorszag
Margitsziget (Európa Ház),
H-1138 BUDAPEST
Fax: (36) 1 111 62 16

IRELAND/IRLANDE
Government Stationery Office
4-5 Harcourt Road, IRL-DUBLIN 2
Fax: (353) 14 75 27 60

ISRAEL/ISRAËL
ROY International
PO Box 13056
IL-61130 TEL AVIV
Fax: (972) 349 78 12

ITALY/ITALIE
Libreria Commissionaria Sansoni
Via Duca di Calabria, 1/1
Casella Postale 552, I-50125 FIRENZE
Fax: (39) 55 64 12 57

MALTA/MALTE
L. Sapienza & Sons Ltd
26 Republic Street
PO Box 36
VALLETTA CMR 01
Fax: (356) 246 182

NETHERLANDS/PAYS-BAS
InOr-publikaties, PO Box 202
NL-7480 AE HAAKSBERGEN
Fax: (31) 542 72 92 96

NORWAY/NORVÈGE
Akademika, A/S Universitetsbokhandel
PO Box 84, Blindern
N-0314 OSLO
Fax: (47) 22 85 30 53

PORTUGAL
Livraria Portugal, Rua do Carmo, 70
P-1200 LISBOA
Fax: (351) 13 47 02 64

SPAIN/ESPAGNE
Mundi-Prensa Libros SA
Castelló 37, E-28001 MADRID
Fax: (34) 15 75 39 98

Llibreria de la Generalitat
Rambla dels Estudis, 118
E-08002 BARCELONA
Fax: (34) 34 12 18 54

SWEDEN/SUÈDE
Aktiebolaget CE Fritzes
Regeringsgatan 12, Box 163 56
S-10327 STOCKHOLM
Fax: (46) 821 43 83

SWITZERLAND/SUISSE
Buchhandlung Heinimann & Co.
Kirchgasse 17, CH-8001 ZÜRICH
Fax: (41) 12 51 14 81

BERSY
Route du Manège 60, CP 4040
CH-1950 SION 4
Fax: (41) 27 31 73 32

TURKEY/TURQUIE
Yab-Yay Yayimcilik Sanayi Dagitim Tic Ltd
Barbaros Bulvari 61 Kat 3 Daire 3
Besiktas, TR-ISTANBUL

UNITED KINGDOM/ROYAUME-UNI
HMSO, Agency Section
51 Nine Elms Lane
GB-LONDON SW8 5DR
Fax: (44) 171 873 82 00

**UNITED STATES and CANADA/
ÉTATS-UNIS et CANADA**
Manhattan Publishing Company
468 Albany Post Road
PO Box 850
CROTON-ON-HUDSON, NY 10520, USA
Fax: (1) 914 271 58 56

STRASBOURG
Librairie Kléber
Palais de l'Europe
F-67075 STRASBOURG Cedex
Fax: (33) 88 52 91 21

Council of Europe Publishing/Editions du Conseil de l'Europe
Council of Europe/Conseil de l'Europe
F-67075 Strasbourg Cedex
Tel. (33) 88 41 25 81 - Fax (33) 88 41 27 80